WORKSKILLS
Book 3

Kathy S. Van Ormer

Consulting Authors

Mary Lou Beilfuss Byrne
Susan C. Quatrini

Library of Congress Cataloging-in-Publication Data

Van Ormer, Kathy S., 1951-
    Workskills. Book 3 / Lathy S. Van Ormer ; consulting authors,
Mary Lou Beilfuss Byrne, Susan C. Quatrini.
        p.   cm.
    ISBN 0-13-953092-4 : $8.50
    1. English language--Textbooks for foreign speakers.   I. Byrne,
Mary Lou Beilfuss, 1954-   . II. Quatrini, Susan C., 1952-   .
III. Title. IV. Title: Workskills book 3. V. Title: Workskills
book three.
PE1128.V34 1994
428.2'4--dc20   93-14196
                                                             CIP

Acquisitions Editor: Nancy Leonhardt
Director of Production and Manufacturing: David Riccardi
Editorial Production/Design Manager: Dominick Mosco
Pre-Press Production: Infinite Graphics
Cover Illustration: Comstock
Cover Design: Laura Ierardi
Cover Design Coordinator: Merle Krumper
Production Coordinator: Ray Keating

The editors have made every effort to trace the
ownership of all copyrighted material and express
regret in advance for any error or omission. After
notification of an oversight, they will include
proper acknowledgement in future printings.

Printed in the United States of America

10   9   8   7

ISBN 0-13-953092-4

Contents

About the Book

Brief Description of *Workskills*

Workskills is a series of three books and three audiotapes for workplace literacy. The books and tapes are written for students at high beginning (Students are literate.), low intermediate, and high intermediate levels. The books and tapes are coordinated so that they can be used with multi-level groups of students and one teacher. Each book deals with different aspects of the same unit topic.

The approach of the texts is functional, contextual, and problem-solving. The exercises are interactive, cooperative, and practical.

Reading, vocabulary development, speaking, listening, and writing are included. The readings are controlled in length and structure. Basic math skills and graphical literacy are included. Positive work attitudes are developed.

Features of *Workskills*

Each unit contains these features:

Before You Read
Reading About Work (a titled story or dialogue based on the unit theme)
Understanding New Words
Understanding the Reading
Discussing
Reading at Work (including Understanding New Words, a nonfictional reading related to types of reading required at work, and Understanding the Reading)
Writing
Listening
Using Math or Using Graphical Literacy

Teaching with *Workskills*

Before You Read

The unit opening page contains one or more photographs, one or more illustrations, or one or more cartoon frames related to the unit theme. Students examine the photos/illustrations/cartoons and describe what they see. The instructor may wish to list vocabulary suggested by the students. The students continue to work with partners to read, think about and answer the questions on the page. This process helps build on existing vocabulary, relates real work experiences to the lesson, and prepares the students for the reading that follows.

Reading About Work

The **Reading About Work** section includes a fictional story or dialogue that follows the **Before You Read** page and illustrates the unit theme. The stories or dialogues proceed from simple sentences, verb tenses, and grammatical structures to more complex sentences, verb tenses, and grammatical structures. The length of the stories or dialogues gradually increases to help students prepare for the succeeding *Workskills* book(s). The authors chose story settings that represent a variety of workplace situations and/or settings that most students would be familiar with.

Understanding New Words

This feature helps expand and use new vocabulary that was introduced in context in the story or dialogue. Various formats were used throughout *Workskills* to help students find, understand, and practice the new or unfamiliar vocabulary. This section can be used successfully either before or after the story or dialogue, depending on the instructor's preference and the needs of the students.

Understanding the Reading

This feature helps both students and teacher check literal and inferential comprehension of the story or dialogue. Once again, various formats were used in *Workskills* to create and maintain interest. These exercises may be done independently as an assessment, or with a partner or a small group, thus providing more speaking practice.

Discussing

The Discussing portion of the unit provides opportunities for the students to work together on specific activities relating to the story or dialogue and to the unit topic. Students may be asked to complete a conversation, to role play situations they may encounter at the workplace, to solve problems, to evaluate and judge reasons for being late for work, to judge appropriate and inappropriate statements in conversations, etc.

Listening

Each unit of *Workskills* includes a listening activity. The conversations that correspond to the listening activities in the books are found on the accompanying audiotapes for *Workskills 1, 2, 3.* The types of conversations included are ones that students might hear at work or participate in at work. Most of the conversations involve two co-workers, a supervisor and a worker, or two supervisors. The conversations involve people discussing work-related topics or making "small talk" at work.

The students' tasks in most cases is to listen for specific information. They will need to use this information for various further activities—to fill in a chart or grid, circle or write an answer, take notes, or make judgments. Many times at work, employees are given information that they need to act on. Thus, in some of the listening activities, the students will use the information for further problem-solving activities.

The speech in the conversations is natural and idiomatic. The students will learn that they don't need to understand every word when they are listening for specific information. The exercises will help train the students to pick out only the information pertinent to the task and will also assist them in understanding spoken English in on-the-job situations.

Reading at Work

The Reading at Work section in each unit focuses on the types of readings that an employee might actually encounter on the job: signs, memos, notices on bulletin boards, excerpts from policy and safety manuals, and excerpts from company newsletters. Many of the readings are authentic—at times, they have been modified for the level of *Workskills* in which they are included.

A variety of comprehension activities follows the readings. These include exercises involving literal and inferential comprehension, making judgments and scanning for specific information. Discussion questions relating the readings to the students' jobs are also included. Whenever possible, the instructor should bring in authentic reading materials from the students' worksite. These added realia will personalize the topic and help the employee to understand his company and his job better.

Writing

These materials are designed to teach English through an integrated skills approach. The writing exercises in the texts generally follow the reading, speaking and listening activities and build upon the previous exercises. The writing exercises are controlled either through format and structure (filling in words, using forms, etc.), or a model is provided with the exercise. Students should be encouraged to draw freely from the model when writing.

The authors also recommend using pre-writing strategies such as brain-storming for ideas and vocabulary, reviewing the reading with a focus on finding specific vocabulary or grammatical structures, group discussion about the writing task, and having the instructor or other class members create a model. The writing assignment may be done as an individual, partner, or group activity.

Using Math and Graphs

The *Workskills* texts include a basic math and graphical skills component in each unit. These exercises were designed to enhance basic skills and meet basic job and personal math needs for the student. The units focus on problems that students will encounter either at work or in their daily lives. Successful completion of all these exercises should prepare students for most basic uses of math in the workplace. Supplemental practice and additional exercises may be necessary for students with limited mathematical background or those who will need a higher level of proficiency on their jobs.

Acknowledgments

We wish to thank the following people:

Elizabeth Minicz
Roseanne Mendoza
Sheila McMillen
Anne Riddick
Rosemary Palicki
Marilyn Antonik

We are also grateful to our students at

Barrett Bindery
C-Line Office Products
College of DuPage
Filtran
Johnson & Quin
Navistar International
Oakton Community College
Panek Precision
Schwake Stone Co.
Triton College

This book is dedicated to my husband, Bill Stump, for his support in all my endeavors and his faith in me.

Special thanks to Van and Gail for being my folks.

UNIT 1   *Company Policies*

Before You Read
(establishing prior knowledge, making predictions)

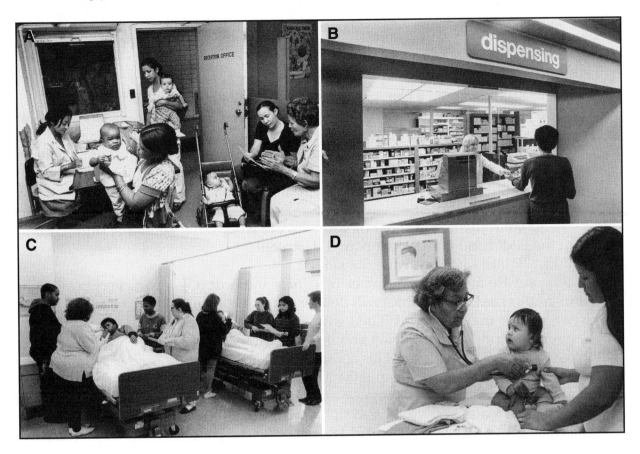

Talk about the photographs with a partner.

Write your responses to the questions.

1. Where are these people?   a. _____

   b. _____   c. _____

   d. _____

2. What is the main idea the photographs represent?

   _____

3. Who pays for health care in this country? _____

4. Who pays for health care in other countries?

   _____

Reading About Work

To Your Health Benefits

The employee lunchroom was crowded, but Benny could see Miriam and Blanca at a table in the corner. They waved to him as he made his way across the room.

"Hi, Benny. You're slow getting here, as usual," Blanca said. "The meeting is already beginning."

Mrs. Perez from the Personnel Department was speaking into a microphone. "May I have your attention, please? I would like to get this meeting started."

The employees directed their eyes toward Mrs. Perez at the front of the room.

"We're here to talk about a change in the company benefits plan," Mrs. Perez began. "We have something new to offer you for your health-care needs. It's called an HMO—that stands for Health Maintenance Organization."

"Oh, good," Miriam whispered. "My sister has been in an HMO for over a year and she really likes it. I've been hoping for the chance to get into one."

"What's the difference between an HMO and. . . " Blanca began.

"Shhh," Benny interrupted.

Mrs. Perez continued. "For those of you who are wondering about the difference between the HMO and our current plan, I'll explain."

"Thanks," Blanca said quietly as she smiled.

"HMOs provide medical care at specific clinics and hospitals," Mrs. Perez said. "Doctors authorized by the HMO will deliver your care. Your current family physician may or may not be affiliated with an HMO. If your doctor is not in an HMO offered by our company plan and if you want to enroll in an HMO, then you will have to select a new doctor. This could be a disadvantage to joining an HMO. The advantage is that in the long run an HMO could cost you less than what you would pay under our other insurance program. Take a look at the information packet you have been given. After you've studied it, I'll answer any questions you have."

"I like this HMO plan," Miriam said after reading the papers. "I think I'm going to sign up."

"Well, I don't know," Blanca sounded doubtful. "My doctor's name isn't on any of these lists and I don't want to change to a doctor I don't even know. I think I'll stay with the old plan. What about you, Benny?"

"I can see good things in both plans," Benny said. "I'm not sure what to do. I think I'll take these papers home and discuss it with my wife."

"That's a good idea, Benny," Blanca said, laughing. "But you'll have to hurry. We have only three weeks to make a decision and you know how slow you are!"

Understanding New Words and Phrases

(learning and using new words and phrases)

Circle the the letter that best describes the underlined word or phrase.

1. The company is offering a change in employee <u>benefits</u>.

    a. work schedules

    b. nonsalary compensation such as medical insurance, paid holidays, and pension plans

2. Some people prefer their <u>HMO</u> to traditional insurance plans.

    a. system of health care delivery and insurance

    b. club for people with the same kind of disease

3. Doctors <u>authorized</u> by the HMO will deliver your health care.

    a. given a legal contract

    b. influenced

4. Your current family doctor may not be <u>affiliated with</u> an HMO.

    a. in approval of

    b. a member of

5. <u>In the long run</u> an HMO could be less expensive than other insurance plans.

    a. in the beginning

    b. over a long period of time

6. Blanca seemed <u>doubtful</u> about the HMO.

    a. uncertain

    b. excited

Understanding the Reading

(checking literal and inferential comprehension)

Read the sentences about the story. Circle *T* for *true* and *F* for *false*. The first one is done for you.

1. The employees had a meeting to discuss problems at work.   *T*   (*F*)

2. Mrs. Perez from the Personnel Department spoke to the employees.   *T*   *F*

3. All the employees knew about HMOs.   *T*   *F*

4. The employees can use any doctor they want if they join the HMO.   *T*   *F*

5. Mrs. Perez told the employees to join the HMO.   *T*   *F*

6. Mrs. Perez said there were advantages and disadvantages to an HMO.   *T*   *F*

7. Miriam is going to join the HMO.   *T*   *F*

8. Blanca joked with Benny about being slow.   *T*   *F*

"It keeps our insurance premiums down."

Discussing

Activity #1 *(critical thinking)*

Work with a partner. Read the description of services for the two dental plans, and decide which plan would be better for you and your family. Explain your reasons to your partner.

(Note: *deductible* is the amount of money you must pay before the insurance company will pay the rest.)

	Dental Plan *A*	Dental Plan *B*
Exams, Cleaning, X-Rays	100%	100%
Other Covered Procedures	50%	50%–80%
Orthodontic Coverage (Braces)	Not covered	Cost to member of $1,250
Maximum per Calender Year	$1,000	Unlimited
Deductible per Person, per Calendar Year	$25.00	None
Claim Forms Required	Yes	No
Dentists	May use any dentist	Must use a plan dentist

Activity #2: Fact or opinion *(critical thinking)*

Discuss the statements with your partner. Write *fact* or *opinion* on the line in front of the statement.

_____ 1. An HMO is better than other medical insurance.

_____ 2. Some insurance plans require you to use certain doctors.

_____ 3. You wait longer for an appointment with an HMO doctor.

_____ 4. One medical insurance may pay for more services than another.

_____ 5. The more expensive an insurance is, the better the service.

_____ 6. People can get medical insurance only through their jobs.

_____ 7. Medical insurance is an important part of an employee's benefit plan.

Writing
(filling out a form)

Your company may require you to give written notification if you want to change your benefits. Use the form below to enroll your family in a new health plan.

To:_____   Date:_____

    Personnel Department

From:_____   RE: Change in Health Benefits

Please enroll _____ in the following health plan (check one):
          (me, my family)

_____ Company Health and Hospital Insurance

_____ Company Health Maintenance Organization

Employee Name: _____

Department: _____

Soc. Sec. #:_____   D.O.B. _____
                                 (month/day/year)

(List names, relationship and birthdates (D.O.B.) of all people to be covered under this plan.)

Name	Relationship	D.O.B
_____	_____	_____
		(mo./day/year)
_____	_____	_____
		(mo./day/year)
_____	_____	_____
		(mo./day/year)
_____	_____	_____
		(mo./day/year)
_____	_____	_____
		(mo./day/year)

Reading at Work

Understanding New Words

(using new words)

1. Your *beneficiaries* are the people you select to receive the income from your insurance policies.

2. *Reimbursement* is paying someone back for something the person already paid for.

3. A *disability* is an inability to continue one's work due to a physical or mental condition.

This is an example of one company's benefit plan.

- Group Life Insurance Benefits—life insurance to protect your beneficiaries.
- Medical Program—financial protection in the event of illness or injury plus a Health Care Program to help you and your family maintain good physical and mental health.
- Reimbursement Account Plan—quarterly employee contributions that you can use to pay unreimbursed medical, dental, and dependent care expenses.
- Disability Income Benefits—protection for you and your family while you are temporarily unable to work, or if you become permanently disabled.
- Pension Plan—company contributions based on salary that will provide retirement benefits.

Understanding the Reading

(checking literal and inferential comprehension)

Discuss these questions in a small group.

1. Are these good benefits? Why or why not?

2. How do these benefits compare to your company's plan? Which is better? Why?

3. If you could add any benefit to your plan, what would it be? Why?

4. If you had to give up one of your current benefits which one would it be? Why?

Listening

(listening for specific information)

A.   An employee has some questions about the form he received from his insurance company. Listen to the telephone conversation and fill in the missing information. Place a check mark (✔) next to information that is written correctly on the form. *(Example:* His name is Francisco Lara.*)*

CLAIM NO	COMPANY NAME		DATE		
025_____	Robertson's _____		7	7	93

EMPLOYEE NAME		SOC. SEC. NUMBER
FRANCISCO LARA ✔		357-09-_____

TYPE OF SERVICE PROVIDER	SERVICE DATES	AMOUNT CHARGED	NOT COVERED	REASON CODE	BASIC PAY	FULL PAY	COVERED MAJ MED.	DEDUCTIBLE	TOTAL PAID
Doctor Visit	06-03-93	25 00							15 00
Minor Surgery	06-03-93	40 00	40 00						-0-

Good Health Insurance Company

The Reason for Amounts Not Covered

DEP –   Dependents Not Coverd
LTR –   Refer To Attached Letter
MAX –   Excess Of Plan Maximum
MSY –   Not A Covered Medical Expense
NRX –   Non Prescription Drug Expenses Not Covered
RPX –   Routine Physical Exams Not Covered
VSN –   Plan Does Not Cover Routine Vision Expense
(Exams, Lens, Frames, Etc.)

B.   Cover the list of reasons. Your teacher will read the letter codes to you. Write the letters on the lines. Check them when you are finished.

1. _____   5. _____

2. _____   6. _____

3. _____   7. _____

4. _____

Using Math
(adding and subtracting decimals)

This is an example of a statement that an insurance company might send to inform you of how much they are paying for your medical services. Add the numbers in the vertical (up and down) columns. As you move horizontally (left to right) in the rows, subtract the "not covered" and "deductible" amounts from the "amount charged." This statement details the amount being sent to Dr. Morales. Put the amount of Dr. Morales's check in the box below his name and address.

CLAIM NO	COMPANY NAME						DATE		
52-27-0	Robertson's Plastics						11	19	93

GROUP	SECTION	CERT NO.	EMPLOYEE NAME				SOC. SEC. NUMBER		
251	701	24270	FRANCISCO LARA				357-09-0245		

TYPE OF SERVICE PROVIDER	SERVICE DATES	AMOUNT CHARGED	NOT COVERED	REASON CODE	BASIC PAY	FULL PAY	COVERED MAJ MED.	DEDUCTIBLE	TOTAL PAID
RX DRUGS	8/31/93	9 20						3 00	
SURG J. MORALES, MD	9/11/93	38 00	12 00						
SURG J. MORALES, MD	10/22/93	30 00						8 50	
OFFICE VISIT J. MORALES, MD	10/29/93	25 00						10 00	
X-RAY PROFESSIONAL LABS	10/29/93	39 00	4 75						
BLOOD TEST PROFESSIONAL LABS	10/29/93	47 75						20 00	
TOTALS >									

Good Health Insurance Company

CHECK >	CHECK REQ. NO.>
JAIME MORALES, MD 110 MAIN STREET MIAMI, FLORIDA	

AMOUNT

UNIT 2 *Giving and Following Directions*

Before You Read
(establishing prior knowledge, making predictions)

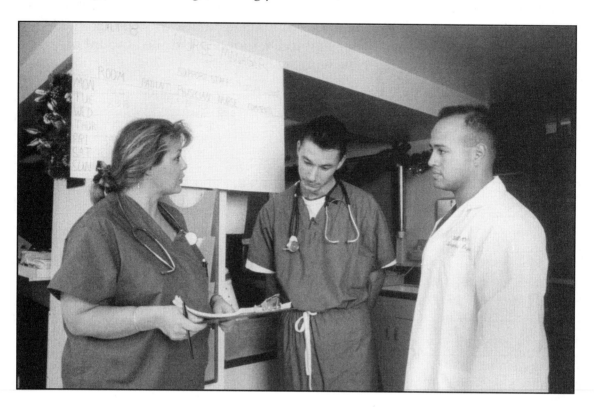

Talk about this photograph with a partner.

Write your responses to the questions.

1. Where are these people? _____

_____

2. What do you think the information on the board tells them? _____

_____

3. What information is on your work schedule? _____

_____

How do you think it is like the schedule in the photograph? _____

_____

How do you think it is different? _____

Reading About Work

Marta's New Job

"Hi, my name is Kenny. I'm going to be training you," Kenny said as he smiled at the new employee.

"Glad to meet you. My name is Marta, and I'm a little nervous. You won't leave me alone, will you? I almost got lost coming to this department." Marta looked a little scared as she and Kenny shook hands.

"Don't worry," Kenny laughed, "we've all had some trouble getting around this place. Especially since it just keeps growing!" Kenny's easy manner relaxed Marta.

"I'll try to relax. Now, show me how to be a fantastic hospital technician." Marta was smiling enthusiastically.

"Well, our job is to go to the patient floors, pick up blood samples, and deliver them to the laboratory. The doctors study the blood tests to learn about the patient's health. Our work is very important and we must follow directions very carefully." Kenny had a serious look on his face now.

Kenny took Marta to the big schedule boards hanging on the wall.

"Since this department is open 24 hours a day, seven days a week, we keep a monthly work schedule for everyone to see. Always check your schedule a month in advance. With so many people, it's difficult to change days off," Kenny said.

"The daily assignments are here on the next board. You must check this as soon as you report for work." Kenny showed Marta where to look. "Normally your assignment will be a particular area of the hospital, such as the second floor, west wing. That's written 2W on the board. You'll have to learn the abbreviations for the units," Kenny said.

Marta knew she would have to concentrate to remember everything Kenny was telling her. Kenny was walking toward the back of the room now.

"This is where you get the basket to carry the blood samples. And over here is where you leave the samples after you have taken them from the patient floors. Before you leave the samples here, you must check the information form on each sample against this checklist. If everything is okay, sign your name at the bottom. If not, fill out the area in the middle of the page that asks you to describe what information is missing. Then, bring this form to the supervisor." Kenny was smiling again. "Seems like a lot, doesn't it? But if you follow directions carefully, it will soon become habit."

"I know I'll be okay after I've practiced a few times. How about letting me show you what I've learned so far?" Marta asked.

"Good idea," Kenny said. "I think you're going to get the hang of this in no time!"

"Sure," Marta joked, "by the end of my shift I may even be able to find my way out of here!"

Understanding New Words and Idioms

(learning and using new words and idioms)

Working with a partner, use the new words and idioms to complete the story below.

get the hang of	habit	concentrate
laboratory technician	abbreviation	enthusiastically
getting around	assignment	manner

Marta was happy with her new job as a _____ in a hospital. The supervisor, Kenny, showed Marta how to read the schedule board. He explained that 2W was an _____ for the west wing of the second floor. Kenny also told Marta about her duties. Marta listened closely because she wanted to _____ as Kenny spoke. She knew that after she had worked here for a while, these duties would become a _____ and then wouldn't seem so difficult. She told Kenny that she was worried about _____ in such a big and confusing hospital. Kenny's calm and relaxed _____ made Marta a little less nervous. Kenny said he was sure that Marta would _____ her new job quickly. Marta responded _____ and wanted to start on her first _____ as soon as possible.

Understanding the Reading

(checking literal and inferential comprehension)

A. Read these sentences with a partner. Decide together whether the statement is true or false. Circle *T* for *true* and *F* for *false.*

1. Marta trained Kenny in his new job.   T   F

2. Marta easily found her way to the department.   T   F

3. Marta's new job was to pick up and deliver blood samples.   T   F

4. Kenny told Marta that the department stays open from 8 A.M. to 8 P.M. Monday through Friday.   T   F

5. A schedule board showed employees' days off for the next month.   T   F

6. A schedule board showed employees where they would work that day.   T   F

7. Marta thought the new job would be easy, so she didn't worry about listening to Kenny.   T   F

B. On the lines below, rewrite the false sentences to make them true. The first one has been done for you. There are three more.

1. Kenny trained Marta in her new job.

_____

_____

_____

_____

_____

Discussing

Activity #1 *(putting things in order)*

Work with your partner, and refer to the reading on page 11. Decide which things on the list are Marta's required daily job duties, and put a check (✔) on the line under *Daily*. Then under the column called *Order,* place the number showing what must be done first, second, and so on. There are six daily duties.

	Daily	Order
Check monthly work schedule.	____	____
Drink morning coffee.	____	____
Get basket for blood samples.	____	____
Check daily work schedule.	____	____
Use car pool to get to work.	____	____
Deliver samples to laboratory.	____	____
Pick up blood samples.	____	____
Pay $1.00 to park car.	____	____
Check information form against checklist.	____	____
Go to assigned unit or units.	____	____

Why must some of Marta's duties be done in a specific order? What could happen if things were done out of order? Why is it important for Marta to check the information form against the checklist?

Activity #2 *(role play, giving directions)*

Work together in pairs. One of you is Partner A and the other is Partner B.

1. Think about the job you have right now. What are some of the things you do every day? What are some of the things you do once a week, or once a month? Try to remember what it was like the first day you started this job. Now pretend Partner A is training a new employee (Partner B) to do this job. What is the first thing you would tell the new employee to do? What's the next step? Continue until you have given the new employee complete instructions about doing your job. When you have finished, change roles so that Partner A is now the new employee and Partner B is doing the training.

2. Now pretend Partner B works in the employment department at your company and must give a new employee directions for getting to this company from at least a mile away. Remember the new employee (Partner A) has never been here before so B must explain things such as what bus to take or where the employees park their cars, what door to enter, where the employment office is located, who to ask for and so on.

    This time when you change roles, use different information where you can, such as coming from a different direction, taking a train or asking for a different person.

Writing
(sequencing, writing about job duties)

Look again at the Discussing activities you did. Think about the things you do on your job and the order in which you do them. Using words of order (first, second, next, then, after that, and so on) write about your job duties. If you only have a few duties, write a second set of instructions about the steps you take getting to work every day.

You may use this description of Marta's job as a model.

Hospital Technician
1.   First, check daily work schedule.
2.   Second, get basket for blood samples.
3.   Third, go to assigned unit.
4.   Next, pick up blood samples.
5.   Then, deliver samples to laboratory.
6.   Finally, check information form against checklist.

_____

_____

_____

_____

_____

_____

_____

_____

_____

Reading at Work

Understanding New Words

(expanding vocabulary)

Read the sentences below. Circle the underlined words in the reading that follows.

1. When you receive an identification card, you should always <u>verify</u> the information. Check to see that your name, address, and date of birth are listed correctly.

2. I need some examples of different handwriting. Could you give me a <u>specimen</u> of yours, please?

The following information is from a hospital training manual.

1. Always wear your picture identification card fastened to your uniform pocket.
2. Always verify patients' names on the specimens you collect. When you sign the list, you are responsibile for the specimens.
3. Handle all specimens with extreme care.
4. In the lab, carefully check that the information card on each specimen is completely filled out.
5. If any information is not complete, fill out the area marked "incomplete information card" and give to the supervisor.
6. Sign your checklist when all information is verified.

Understanding the Reading

(checking literal and inferential comprehension)

Discuss the following questions in a small group.

1. Why is it important to do these steps in this order?
2. What could happen if a technician didn't follow instructions?
3. Think about your job. What could happen if you didn't follow directions carefully?

Listening

(listening for specific information)

A. Below is a floor plan of Marta's hospital. Listen to the audiotape to hear the
    instructions Marta received to find the units she was assigned. Fill in the
    blanks showing where she worked each day. (First, locate Marta's laboratory
    on the third floor of the Center Building. That is where Marta started from
    each day.)

1. Monday   _____

2. Tuesday   _____

3. Wednesday   _____

4. Thursday   _____

5. Friday   _____

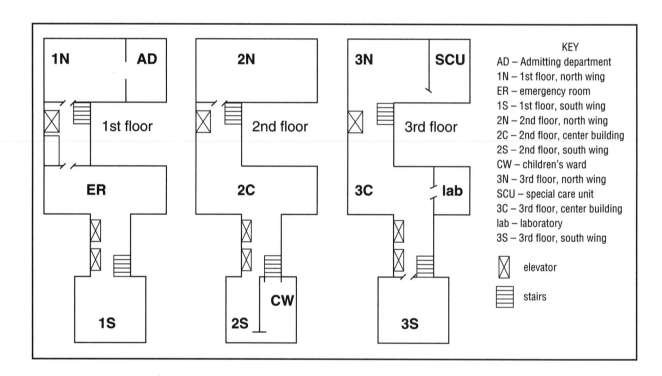

B. With a partner, practice giving directions to the units shown in the floor
    plan. Take turns giving directions and telling which unit was reached.

Using Charts and Forms
(filling out charts and forms)

Work with a partner. Partner A will look at the schedule on this page and
Partner B will look at the schedule on the next page. Complete the schedule
for Marta and her co-workers by asking each other questions such as
"When are Peter's days off?" and "Where is Irene assigned on Tuesday?"
The abbreviations for the units correspond to the floor plan on page 18.

	Mon	Tue	Wed	Thu	Fri	Sat	Sun
Kenny		3N 3C, 3S		2C, 2N 1S	SCU, 2S, CW		off
Irene	off		1S, 2C, 2N	ER, 1N		1N ER, 1S	
Robert	2N, 2C 2S, CW			off		3N, SCU 3C, 3S	
Peter			SCU 2S, CW				2N, 2C 2S, CW
Marta	1N ER, 1S	ER, 1N			1S 2C, 2N	off	

The following are information cards placed on the blood samples. Work with your
partner as you did above to complete the cards.

Date of sample __August 10, 1992__   Time taken _____

Patient's name __Brandon, Mary__   ID # _____

Doctor's name _____   ID # __9301__

Test Codes — Check all that apply.

☐ A1   ☑ A2   ☐ B1   ☐ B2   ☐ C1   ☐ C2   ☐ All

Date of sample _____   Time taken __12:15 pm__

Patient's name _____   ID # __990135__

Doctor's name __Dr. L. Gonzalez__   ID # _____

Test Codes — Check all that apply.

☑ A1   ☐ A2   ☑ B1   ☐ B2   ☐ C1   ☐ C2   ☐ All

Work with a partner. Partner B will look at the schedule on this page and Partner A will look at the schedule on page 19. Complete the schedule chart for Marta and her co-workers by asking each other questions such as "When is Robert's other day off?" and "Where is Marta assigned on Monday?" The abbreviations for the units correspond to the floor plan on page 18.

B

	Mon	**Tue**	**Wed**	**Thu**	**Fri**	**Sat**	**Sun**
Kenny	3N, SCU 3C, 3S		ER, 1N			off	
Irene		off			3S 3C, 3N		3N, SCU 3C, 3S
Robert		SCU 2S, CW	off		ER, 1N		
Peter	off	1S 2C, 2N		3S, 3C, 3N		2N, 2C 2S, CW	
Marta			3S 3C, 3N	SCU 2C, CW			off

The following are information cards placed on the blood samples. Work with your partner as you did above to complete the cards.

Date of sample _____   Time taken _7:30 am_

Patient's name _____   ID # _735264_

Doctor's name _Dr. D. Martin_____   ID # _____

Test Codes — Check all that apply.

☐ A1   ☐ A2   ☑ B1   ☐ B2   ☐ C1   ☐ C2   ☐ All

Date of sample _August 11, 1992_____   Time taken _____

Patient's name _Randolf, William_____   ID # _____

Doctor's name _____   ID # _4712_

Test Codes — Check all that apply.

☐ A1   ☐ A2   ☐ B1   ☐ B2   ☐ C1   ☑ C2   ☐ All

UNIT 3 *Safety*

Talk about the photographs with a partner.

Write your responses to the questions.

1. What do these photographs show? _____

    _____

    What do they have in common? _____

2. What special equipment is used where you work? _____

    _____

    What signs have you seen at work? _____

    _____

Reading About Work

Andy Learns About OSHA

The cafeteria was busy and noisy, as usual. The low buzz of people talking was mixed with the sound of dishes hitting together.

"Half the factory must eat at 11:45 every day," Andy mumbled to himself.

People were lined up along the food tables, choosing salads, fruits, and vegetables along with the main dish.

"Meat loaf—again?" Andy complained.

Ahead of him were two men wearing name tags marked "Visitors—OSHA".

"We're almost through," one man was saying. "Just the air tests and storage areas left."

"Yes," the other man responded. "Things have gone pretty well here. We should be back in the office by tomorrow."

As they moved on down the line, Andy wondered what the men were talking about. And what was that word on their name tags? OSHA?

Andy paid the cashier and then saw Sergio sitting at a nearby table. Sergio was a foreman with 16 years experience. Maybe he could answer Andy's questions.

"Is this seat taken?" Andy asked.

"No. Sit down, Andy. I was just starting lunch myself," Sergio answered.

"Sergio," Andy began, "did you see those two men who were in front of me?"

"You mean the OSHA guys?" Sergio asked.

"Yeah—what's OSHA, anyway? And what do they want with our air and storage areas?" Andy seemed very interested.

"OSHA stands for *Occupational Safety and Health Administration*. It's part of the U.S. Department of Labor and is responsible for assuring that employers provide a safe workplace for employees," Sergio explained.

Andy was beginning to get the picture.

"So, OSHA wants to take air samples and check storage areas to make sure that employees here won't get sick from the chemicals, is that it?" Andy asked.

"That's right." Sergio continued. "As a printing company, we work with a lot of inks, dyes, and cleaning chemicals that are potentially hazardous. The employees must know the proper use and handling of those chemicals. Our management must see that we are well trained and have safe places for storage and disposal. The company, or any employee, can ask for an OSHA inspection if there is any concern about employee safety."

"Does OSHA inspect only factories? My brother works in construction and that seems pretty dangerous to me." Andy sounded a little worried.

"OSHA is everywhere there are jobs and people working those jobs," Sergio reassured him. "There are special rules for every industry and stiff fines and penalties for employers who don't comply with the regulations."

"Hey, those men are leaving. Do you think I could watch them test the air?" Andy eagerly ate his lunch.

"I don't see why not, it's still your lunch time." Sergio laughed. "That's the first time in 16 years I've seen anyone eat this meat loaf with such enthusiasm!"

Understanding New Words and Idioms
(learning and using new words and idioms)

A. Read the sentences with a partner. Decide together whether *a* or *b* is most like the numbered statement. Circle *a* or *b*.

1. People were <u>lined up</u> along the food tables.
   a. People stood in back of each other beside the food tables.
   b. People stood beside each other and made a circle around the food tables.
2. Andy was <u>beginning to get the picture</u>.
   a. Andy was starting to understand.
   b. Andy was going to buy a painting.
3. Employees at this company handle <u>potentially hazardous</u> chemicals.
   a. Employees use chemicals that are completely safe.
   b. Employees use chemicals that could cause illness or injury if not used correctly.
4. Employers could be made to pay <u>stiff fines and penalties</u>.
   a. Employers could have to pay a lot of money as punishment.
   b. Employers could have to pay higher taxes as punishment.

B. With your partner, match the words in the box to their definitions. Write the correct word on the line.

mumble	OSHA	occupation
assure	comply	eagerly

_____ 1. to make certain that something will happen

_____ 2. job or work

_____ 3. to speak unclearly or quietly

_____ 4. showing interest

_____ 5. Occupational Safety and Health Administration

_____ 6. to obey a rule or regulation

C. Using the same words, complete the sentences below.

   1. If a company doesn't _____ with _____ regulations, the

      company could be fined.

   2. On Friday afternoon the employees _____ waited for their

      paychecks.

   3. "Let me _____ you," the boss said. "Good work will always be

      rewarded."

   4. If your _____ is actor, teacher, or politician, you must learn to speak

      clearly and not _____.

Understanding the Reading

(checking literal and inferential comprehension)

Work in a group of three or four students. Read the statements below and decide together whether to put a check (✔) under the column for *agree* or *disagree*.

		agree	disagree
1.	OSHA inspectors can check for clean air and proper storage areas.	_____	_____
2.	OSHA inspections are done only where there are chemicals being used.	_____	_____
3.	An employer or an employee can ask for an OSHA inspection.	_____	_____
4.	It is the employer's responsibility to train employees to work safely.	_____	_____
5.	If an accident happens at work, it's never the employee's fault.	_____	_____
6.	The federal government doesn't get involved in worker safety.	_____	_____
7.	If a company doesn't know it's doing something wrong, it doesn't have to pay the fine.	_____	_____
8.	Employees should always let the employer decide what is safe or not safe and never get involved.	_____	_____

Discussing

Activity #1: Role Play *(problem solving, making predictions)*

Work with a partner.

1. Partner A is the supervisor. The safety record for A's employees is very good, but A can be difficult about accidents. Partner A believes that most accidents are caused by employee carelessness and poor attention to detail. Before the shift began, A was told by his or her boss that production is behind schedule and they have got to make it up.

    Partner B is the employee. At the beginning of the shift, B notices the equipment he or she is using isn't working correctly. It continues to run, but it gives off little sparks every few minutes. B reports the problem to A, but A doesn't want to lose production time by shutting the machine down.

Act out the conversation that takes place between A and B giving as many reasons for each side as you can.

2. Reverse roles so that A is the employee and B is the supervisor. Now pretend it is two hours into the shift. Partner A just got a bad burn on the arm and is reporting it to B. What do they say to each other?

With the whole group, talk about what an employee can do if a supervisor refuses to get the equipment fixed.

Activity # 2 *(critical thinking)*

Here are some safety rules. With a partner, discuss the reason for the rule. Share your answers with the group.

1. Work areas should have plenty of fresh air.

    Reason:_____

2. Work areas should have good lighting.

    Reason:_____

3. Machines should have safety guards around moving parts.

    Reason:_____

4. Machines should have an easy to reach *on–off* switch.

    Reason:_____

5. Equipment and supplies should be stored away from busy work areas.

    Reason:_____

6. Hazardous chemicals must have clearly marked warnings.

    Reason:_____

7.   Always clean up spills.

Reason:_____

8.   Know where fire exits are located.

Reason:_____

9.   Life jackets shall be provided for employees working over or near water.

Reason:_____

10.   Worn or frayed electrical cords must not be used.

Reason:_____

Writing
(problem-solving)

The left side of this chart lists some common safety problems. With a partner, discuss how to correct the problem and then write your suggestions in the space on the right.

Safety Problems   **Suggestions**

Safety Problems	Suggestions
Liquid spilled on floor	Clean it up with a mop or a cloth. Or call the housekeeping department.
Supplies stored in hallway	
Overloaded electrical outlet	
Desk drawers left open	
Overly tired employee	
Employees running in work area	

Reading at Work

Understanding New Words

(learning and using new words)

Read the sentences. Find and circle the underlined words in the reading that follows.

1. Ingestion (swallowing) of toxic (poisonous) liquids is very dangerous.

2. Upon inhalation (breathing in), the lungs fill with air.

3. His clothes were contaminated (soiled) by chemicals.

The following is an example of information that OSHA requires employers to tell employees who handle chemicals.

PRODUCT CODE HC-1357

Effects of Exposure

Eye:	Irritation. May injure eye tissue.
Skin:	Irritation, dryness, rash.
Inhalation:	May cause headaches and dizziness.
Ingestion:	Mildly toxic.

First Aid Procedure

Eye:	Wash immediately for at least 15 minutes. Get medical attention.
Skin:	Remove contaminated clothing, wash.
Inhalation:	Fresh air. Get medical attention.
Ingestion:	Get immediate medical attention.
	DO NOT give anything by mouth.

Understanding the Reading

(checking literal and inferential comprehension, problem solving)

Discuss the following questions in a small group.

1. If you got splashed in the face and eyes with this chemical, how would your eyes look? How would they feel? How would the skin on your face look? What should you do?

2. If you accidentally drank this chemical, would it be okay to take a medicine to make you throw up? Why or why not?

3. How would you feel if you breathed this chemical?

Listening

Activity #1 *(listening for specific information)*

In the Reading at Work section, you discussed the harmful effects and first aid procedures for Product HC-1357. Now, listen to the tape to hear the recommendations for protective equipment for workers who handle HC-1357. Put the information in the chart below.

	Protective Equipment and Requirements
Eyes	
Hands	
Skin	
Other	

Activity #2 *(listening and correcting errors)*

Employers are required to fill out accident report forms like the one below. Some of the information on this form is incorrect. Listen to the tape and correct the form by writing the correct answers above the incorrect ones.

REPORT OF EMPLOYEE INJURY

Name of injured: Betty Brown

Employee #: 711590

Department: Housekeeping

Job title: House keeper

About the Injury

Occurred: ___ on ✓ off duty

Location: Main Lobby

Date: 9/12/93 Time: 8:00 PM

Description of accident or injury   Employee cut right hand on a piece of tin
while emptying a wastebasket.

Using Math and Charts
(adding and subtracting decimals, reading and interpreting charts, problem solving)

The U.S. Department of Labor keeps records of all job-related accidents and illnesses that occur each year. A chart of this information would be similar to the one shown here. The industries are listed in the column on the left. On the right are the number of incidents reported for every 100 workers.

Reports of Occupational Accidents and Injuries	
Industry	**Total Cases per 100 workers**
Agriculture & Fishing	11.4
Mining	8.4
Construction	15.2
Manufacturing	10.4
Transportation & Utilities	8.5
Wholesale & Retail Trade	7.4
Finance & Real Estate	2.0
Service	5.4
Other	7.9

Using Decimals
The dot in *11.4* is called a decimal point. The first place to the right of the decimal point represents "tenths"; 11.4 is read *eleven and four tenths*. Read the numbers on the chart to your partner. Then listen as your partner reads the numbers to you.

Adding Decimals
1. Put the numbers to be added in a column. Line up the decimal points. The numbers to the right of the decimal point are less than 1. Whole numbers are on the left of the decimal point
2. Add. (You may need to "carry.") Keep the decimal point in the answer in line with the decimal points above it.

Example:
```
  11.4
   8.4
  15.2
+ 10.4
------
  45.4
```

Using figures from the chart, practice adding decimals.

Add:
1. Agriculture & Fishing plus Finance & Real Estate.
2. Transportation & Utilities plus Manufacturing.
3. Wholesale & Retail Trade plus Construction.

1. 11.4
   + 2.0
   ____

2. +____

3. +____

Subtracting Decimals

1. Keep the decimal point in line as you did when you were adding. Put the larger number on top.
2. Subtract. (You may need to "borrow.") As in adding, make sure to keep the decimal point in the answer in line with the decimal points above it.

Examples:

```
          7
 11.4    8̸.̸5
- 8.4   - 7.9
 ────    ────
  3.0      .6
```

Using figures from the chart, practice subtracting decimals.

Subtract:

1. Construction minus Mining.
2. Services minus Finance & Real Estate.
3. Manufacturing minus Other.

```
1.  15.2        2.              3.
   - 8.4           -              -
   ──────          ─────          ─────
```

Work with a partner to answer the questions.

1. Which industry reported the most cases of accidents and injuries?

   _____ The least? _____

2. What is the difference between cases reported for Construction and

   Finance? _____

   Which industry would probably be safer for workers?

   _____

3. What is the difference between cases reported for Mining and those reported for Transportation & Utilities?

   _____

   Do you think one is safer than the other? _____

   Which one? _____ Why? _____

4. If a retail trade store had 300 employees, about how many cases would they have reported according to this chart?

   _____

UNIT 4 *Interacting with Co-workers*

Before You Read
(understanding nonverbal behavior, establishing prior knowledge)

Talk about this photograph with a partner.

Write your responses to the questions.

1. Where are these people? _____

   _____

2. What are they doing? _____

   _____

3. What is the mood of the people? _____

   _____

4. The man in the back is sitting alone. He is not smiling or talking. How do

   you think he feels? _____

   _____

   Why? _____

Reading About Work

Table Talk

Kelly put her money in the vending machine and hoped that this time, the cup would drop down before the coffee.

"Oh good," Kelly said to Sylvia, who was standing behind her. "I just hate going to the office to try to get my money back when all I want to do is sit down and enjoy my break."

"It is nice to relax for a few minutes of pleasant conversation, isn't it?" Sylvia said. "Would you like to join Rafael and me? We're sitting right over there." Sylvia pointed to a table nearby.

"Well, if you don't mind . . ." Kelly began, "but, if you would rather talk privately, I'll understand."

Sylvia took Kelly by the arm and walked toward the table where Rafael was sitting.

"Rafael," Sylvia said, "do you mind if Kelly joins us?"

"Of course not," Rafael answered. "Kelly, why do you seem so hesitant to join us? Do you think we're unfriendly?"

"It's not that," Kelly said. "It's just that usually when I see you two together, you aren't speaking English. It makes me feel, well . . . like you don't want me to know what you are saying."

"Oh no, Kelly!" Sylvia looked very surprised. "We don't mean that, at all! I'm sorry if we ever made you feel bad. It certainly wasn't our intention, was it, Rafael?"

"Absolutely not, Kelly," Rafael said. "I apologize, too."

"Oh, I didn't think you intentionally tried to make me feel like an outsider. Actually, you've been very nice to me. Not like that group from Maintenance over there." Kelly pointed to several people at a table across the room.

"They're downright rude!" Kelly said. "I said 'Hi' as I walked past them when I went to get my coffee, and they just looked at me. Then one of them said something in their native language and everyone laughed." Kelly looked upset.

"Kelly, I don't know what they said, but it could have been just a misunderstanding, you know," Rafael said, trying to console Kelly.

"I suppose you're right, but it's hard not to be offended sometimes," Kelly said.

"I know what you mean, Kelly," Sylvia agreed. "Actually, I like it when we speak English at work because the only way to really learn English is to use it! Also, I like to listen to the things Americans talk about—and don't talk about!"

"What do you mean—the things we don't talk about?" Kelly was puzzled.

"Well, for instance, money . . ." Sylvia began.

"Right!" Rafael jumped into the conversation. "Americans like to talk about money, but there are certain questions that are considered rude. Such as asking how much money they earn, or how much they paid for their house or car."

"Unless, of course, we're bragging about what a discount we got on something!" Kelly said with a laugh.

Understanding New Words and Idioms

(learning and using new words and idioms)

A. Work with a partner. Cross out the word in each group that has a different meaning from the others.

1. dangerous   hesitant   cautious
2. rude   friendly   impolite
3. outsider   stranger   friend
4. dislike   console   comfort
5. offend   insult   ignore
6. brag   shy   boast
7. expensive   discount   price cut

B. With your partner, look at the underlined words in the sentences. Decide whether *a* or *b* is a good description of the word or idiom. Circle *a* or *b*.

1. Kelly thought the employees from Maintenance were <u>downright</u> rude.
   a. completely or thoroughly
   b. under or below

2. Kelly was <u>puzzled by</u> something Sylvia said.
   a. upset about; angry about
   b. uncertain about; not sure about

3. Rafael <u>jumped into the conversation</u>.
   a. began talking before the other person finished talking
   b. walked away before the other person finished talking

4. Rafael <u>apologized</u> to Kelly.
   a. said he was sorry
   b. gave a present

"Show off!"

Understanding the Reading

(checking literal and inferential comprehension)

Work with a partner and decide together how to answer the questions.
Circle *Yes* or *No*.

1. Has Kelly ever lost money in the vending machines at work?	*Yes*	*No*
2. Was Sylvia joining Rafael for break?	*Yes*	*No*
3. Does Kelly try to be friendly?	*Yes*	*No*
4. Did Kelly think Rafael and Sylvia were unfriendly?	*Yes*	*No*
5. Has Kelly ever felt like an outsider?	*Yes*	*No*
6. Does Sylvia like to speak English at work?	*Yes*	*No*
7. Do the employees from Maintenance speak English to Kelly?	*Yes*	*No*
8. Does Rafael know how to talk about money with Americans?	*Yes*	*No*
9. Is it polite to ask someone how much money he earns?	*Yes*	*No*
10. Are some Americans proud of themselves when they buy something for a lower price?	*Yes*	*No*

Discussing

Activity #1: Role play

(problem solving and empathizing)

1. Work in groups of four. You have each won some money. One person won $100, another person won $1000, a third person won $10,000, and the fourth person won $1 million. With this money, each of you may buy only one thing for yourself, and you must buy something for everyone in the class. You should try to choose something you think each person would like. Don't forget to budget your winnings so you'll have enough to buy something for everyone.

2. Work in groups of four. In each group, choose one person who will not participate in the conversation. The other three people will discuss things such as favorite movies, favorite vacations, favorite restaurants, what they did over the past weekend, or other topics that come up in normal conversation. The person who is not participating will be called the *odd-person out* or *OPO*. The OPO must listen to the conversation, but can not talk. The others in the group will talk freely with each other but must not even look at OPO. After five minutes of conversation, change the topic and the OPO. Each person in the group must experience being the OPO. After everyone has had a turn, discuss how you felt when you were OPO.

Activity #2 *(evaluating appropriate behavior)*

Read the statements and discuss them with your partner. Decide which things are *always* appropriate to do, *sometimes* appropriate to do, or *never* appropriate to do. Put a check mark (✔) in the column for *always, sometimes* or *never.*

	Always	Sometimes	Never
1. Tell your co-workers how much money you got in your raise.	—	—	—
2. Tell your closest friend at work how much money you earn.	—	—	—
3. Talk to your supervisor about giving you a raise.	—	—	—
4. Tell your co-workers how much rent you pay every month.	—	—	—
5. Tell your co-workers how much money you saved by shopping at a discount store.	—	—	—
6. Talk to your co-workers about how high your taxes are.	—	—	—
7. Tell your co-workers how much money you got back from your income tax last year.	—	—	—
8. Tell your co-workers how much money your family spends on presents for you.	—	—	—
9. Tell your closest friend at work how much money you have in the bank.	—	—	—
10. Tell your co-workers what you would do with the money if you won the lottery.	—	—	—

Discuss your answers with the whole class. For questions that you answered "sometimes appropriate," talk about what it is in the situation that makes it okay or not okay to talk about.

For example, in the first question, if it was a union raise then all your co-workers would already know about it. But if you aren't in a union job and raises are different for everyone, then it probably isn't a good idea to tell how much your raise was.

For further discussion, talk about these questions with the whole class:
1. Someone asks you a question about money that you don't want to answer. What would you do or say?
2. Has this ever happened to you?
3. What was the question?
4. What did you say to the person who asked you?

Writing
(evaluating appropriate behaviors)

In the reading on page 32 of this unit, you read about people using languages other than English while at work. On this page, you're going to write about your opinion of this subject. The first sentence of each paragraph has been started for you. Here is an example: It is appropriate to speak English at work when I am participating in a public conversation.

It is appropriate to speak English at work when _____

_____

_____

_____

_____

_____

_____

_____

It is appropriate to speak my native language at work when _____

_____

_____

_____

_____

_____

_____

_____

Reading at Work

Understanding New Words

(learning and using new words)

Read the sentences below. Circle the underlined words in the reading that follows.

1. Someone who buys products to use is called a <u>consumer</u>.

2. An <u>association</u> is a group of people organized for a common purpose, such as the Parent-Teacher Association (PTA) at most schools.

3. The Red Cross is <u>dedicated to</u>, or works for the purpose of, helping people in times of emergency.

4. A labor union has <u>negotiated</u> a new contract. That means the union talked with the company to arrange for a pay raise or other changes at work.

5. <u>Retailers</u>—such as grocers, jewelers, and bakers—sell products directly to the users.

6. A good deal on a car means you buy it cheaply and <u>save yourself a bundle</u>.

Many companies offer employees the opportunity to join a buying service like the one described in the following reading. Buying services are also available through other organizations, such as credit unions and motor clubs.

An Important Message for Members of Consumer Buying Association

You are a member of an association that is dedicated to saving money. Consumer Buying Association (CBA) has negotiated with car dealers and retailers to give CBA members special savings on cars, appliances, furniture, and other products and services. The savings could total thousands of dollars!

Here's What You Do

Before you make any major purchases, call CBA. If you are looking for a car, tell us the make and model. For other purchases, just tell us the item. Then we'll send you a CBA purchasing form with the name of the retailer or dealer closest to you. Take the form to the seller—and save yourself a bundle!

- American cars only $100 over factory price

- Furniture at 5% over cost

- TVs, stereos, appliances—up to 50% savings

- Services such as travel, insurance, motor club

Understanding the Reading

(checking literal and inferential comprehension)

In a small group, discuss these questions.

1. What kinds of things can a person buy through CBA?
2. How do you use CBA?
3. Why do you think people want to use a buying service?
4. How does a buying service get retailers and dealers to give them lower prices?
5. Would you use CBA? What would you buy?

Listening

Activity #1 *(listening for an appropriate response)*

Work with a partner. Listen to the audiotaped conversation that goes with each picture. For each conversation, choose an appropriate response. Circle *a, b,* or *c.*

a. Gee, I really feel uncomfortable talking about that. Let's talk about something else.
b. If you are so interested, why don't you go ask the Vice President of Personnel.
c. I don't remember what I'm making.

a. $15 thousand.
b. Aren't you being rather nosy?
c. I'd rather not say. I wouldn't want people to think I was bragging.

Frank Labua

Frank Labua

3.

a. I don't really think it's any of your business and, besides, I hate people who gossip.

b. Let's not spread a story that may not be true, okay?

c. It's got to be at least $200, if not more!

4.

a. That's right. Who do they think they are—trying to change us and make us forget our own heritage?

b. Well, I guess we have to do it because we are only employees and the company can fire us if we don't.

c. I think we should speak English at work because this is our country now. We need to know English, so we can make a good life here.

Activity #2 (listening for specific information and checking information)

Informal communication at work is known as "the grapevine." In this activity, you will work in groups of four to pass a message. One of you will listen to the message on the audiotape while the other three wait where they can't hear the tape. Then, the first person will whisper the message to the second person. The second person whispers the message to the third, and the third to the fourth. The fourth person must repeat the message to the whole class. Then, play the tape to hear the original message. The whole class should compare the "grapevine" messages with the original.

Using Math

(converting decimals and percents, problem solving)

Solve the following problems to see how much money Kelly's co-workers have saved when they've bought things on sale and at discount stores.

You will need to know how to change percents to decimals. The rule is: *Remove the percent sign and divide the number by 100.*

Examples

$$30\% = \frac{.3}{100\overline{)30.0}}$$
$$\underline{300}$$

$$75.5\% = \frac{.755}{100\overline{)75.500}}$$
$$\underline{700}$$
$$550$$
$$\underline{500}$$
$$500$$
$$\underline{500}$$

Practice

$$15\% = 100\overline{)15.00}$$

$$43.75\% =$$

$$82\% =$$

A quick way to change percents to decimals is: *Remove the percent sign and move the decimal point two places to the left.*

Examples

$$7.5\% = .075 \text{ or } .075 \qquad 98\% = .98 \text{ or } .98$$

Practice

$$11.5\% = \qquad 53\% = \qquad 67\% =$$

Problems

1. During a special 10%-off sale, Lupe bought a sofa that was regularly $399. How much did the sofa cost? _____ How much is the 7% sales tax on the sofa? _____ What is the final cost of the sofa plus tax? _____

2. Mikhail found a discount store where he could buy a washing machine for $459 and the matching dryer for 85% of the cost of the washing machine. How much was the dryer? _____ What was the total price for the two appliances? _____

3. Eva joined a discount travel club that promises a 35% rebate on all cruises. She and her husband have purchased cruise tickets for $1,999 each. How much will the couple get back on both tickets together? _____ After the rebate, what did each ticket cost? _____

4. Andre wanted to buy a car that had a list price of $15,750. He bought the car through a buying service that gave him an 8% discount. How much money did he save? _____ What was the price of the car after the discount? _____

5. The Chins are redecorating their house. They need paint, brushes, wallpaper, and some tools that will cost a total of $217. When they got to the hardware store, they found the store was having a 25% off sale. How much money did they save? _____ How much did the supplies cost them with the discount? _____

In the following problems, change interest rates (percents) to decimals and solve.

6. To buy his car, Andre took out a loan for $4,750 at 11.5% per year. He plans to pay off the loan in one year. How much money in interest will he have paid at the end of the year? _____

7. Magda put $1,000 of her savings into a 12-month Certificate of Deposit (CD). The CD is paying 8.75% interest annually. How much money will Magda's CD have earned at the end of one year? _____

8. Magda left $1,000 in her savings account that is paying 5.5% interest per year. How much money will Magda's savings account have earned at the end of one year? _____ How much more will the CD earn than the savings account? _____

UNIT 5 *Interacting with Supervisors*

Before You Read
(establishing prior knowledge)

Talk about this photograph with a partner.

Write your responses to the questions.

1. Which person is the supervisor?_____

   _____

2. Which person is the employee? _____

   _____

3. How do they feel about working together? _____

   Explain your answer. _____

   _____

Reading About Work

A Big Misunderstanding

"Customer Service Department. My name is Carmen. How may I help you?" Carmen tried to sound friendly, but her heart wasn't in it. She was still thinking about her talk with Mrs. Green, the supervisor.

"She must think I don't know my job," Carmen thought to herself. "Why else would she check on my work and ask me all those questions?"

Carmen noticed the silence on the phone and said, "Hello, hello . . . are you still there?"

"Yes, I am, young lady, but apparently you're not. May I speak to your supervisor, please?" the man asked.

"Oh, I'm sorry. Please let me to try to help you," Carmen said.

"I wish to speak to Mrs. Green," he repeated.

"Certainly. Just a moment, please." Carmen connected the man to Mrs. Green's phone line.

"Well, now I've done it," Carmen said under her breath. "This man's complaint will convince Mrs. Green that I don't know my job."

Within a minute, Mrs. Green asked Carmen to come into her office.

"Carmen, about that last call . . ." Mrs. Green began.

"I'm sorry, Mrs. Green, but I've just been so worried since our talk," Carmen interrupted. "All day, I've been thinking about what I could have done to make you check on me and ask me all those questions."

"Carmen, please, calm down," Mrs. Green was smiling now. "I'm surprised you think I'm unhappy with your work. I have often told you how much I rely on you. Why didn't you tell me you were upset about our talk? I could have put your mind at ease."

"Well, I guess I didn't think I should take up your time with my little problems," Carmen said.

"It's not a little problem if it bothers you this much," Mrs. Green replied. "Carmen, I would like to see you advance in this company. I asked you questions because I wanted to know how you would handle the kinds of problems you might have in a higher position."

"Oh. Well, what do you think of my problem solving abilities, now?" Carmen asked.

Mrs. Green laughed. "Well, mostly your judgment is very good. But I hope you have learned something, Carmen. Don't ever hesitate to talk to your supervisor about a problem."

"You're absolutely right, Mrs. Green. I never again want to feel like I did today." Carmen relaxed a little.

"Now back to what I was saying about that phone call . . ." Mrs. Green began. "That was Mr. Singh from the training department. I've asked to have you participate in the company's training program. It will prepare you for future promotions. Carmen, you have a funny look on your face. What's the matter?" Mrs. Green asked.

"I was just thinking, after the way I handled that phone call today, maybe I should change my name before I meet Mr. Singh. I wouldn't want him to question your judgment!" Carmen said with a grin.

Understanding New Words and Idioms

(learning and using new words and idioms)

Read the following sentences. Match sentences in the *a–f* list that have the same ideas as those in the *1–6* list. Write the matching sentence on the line.

a. Carmen is concerned about whether Mrs. Green thinks Carmen can take care of problems at work.

b. Carmen wanted to be nice to others, but she was worried about herself.

c. Usually Carmen makes good decisions.

d. Mrs. Green could have explained things so Carmen wouldn't worry.

e. The man thought Carmen wasn't paying attention.

f. Mrs. Green depends on Carmen to do good work.

1. Carmen tried to sound friendly, but her heart wasn't in it.

   _____

2. "I'm here, but apparently you're not," the man said to Carmen.

   _____

3. "I've often told you how much I rely on you," Mrs. Green said to Carmen.

   _____

4. "I could have put your mind at ease," Mrs. Green told Carmen.

   _____

5. "What do you think of my problem-solving abilities, now?" Carmen asked.

   _____

6. "Mostly, your judgment is very good," Mrs. Green told Carmen.

   _____

Understanding the Reading

(checking literal and inferential comprehension)

Match the beginning of the sentence in Column A with the end of the sentence in Column B. Write the completed sentences on the lines.

Column A	Column B
1. Carmen was upset about	into her office.
2. "Mrs. Green must be unhappy	a special training program.
3. Mrs. Green called Carmen	a talk she had with her supervisor.
4. Mrs. Green told Carmen she wanted	whenever there's a problem at work.
5. Mrs. Green recommended Carmen for	with my work," Carmen thought.
6. Carmen learned she should talk to her supervisor	to see Carmen advance in the company.

1. _____

    _____.

2. _____

    _____.

3. _____

    _____.

4. _____

    _____.

5. _____

    _____.

6. _____

    _____.

Discussing

Activity #1: Role play *(using spoken language, problem solving)*

Work with a partner. Partner A is the employee and Partner B is the supervisor. Act out what each of you would say in the following situations.

1. The employee thinks he or she has too much work and is afraid that the quality of work is suffering as a result.
2. The employee thinks he or she has too little work and wants to take on more responsibility.
3. The employee is having a personal problem that is affecting his or her work. The employee wants to discuss it with the supervisor before the supervisor takes any action against the employee.

(Change roles so that both partners play both roles.)

With the class, discuss how you felt about talking to the supervisor in each of the situations above. Were some things easier for you to express than others? Which were easier? Which were more difficult? Did you feel you were able to be direct and come to the point or did you feel you had to be very careful about the words you used to explain your feelings?

Activity #2: *(examining verbal and non-verbal communication)*

Work with your partner to classify the items listed below into things that encourage or discourage communication between people. Write *encourage* in front of the items that encourage communication and *discourage* in front of the items that discourage communications.

1. _____ "It would be best for you if . . ."
2. _____ "Here's the right thing to do . . ."
3. _____ "Tell me about what happened."
4. _____ The listener is silent.
5. _____ "You had better do this or else."
6. _____ "You're wrong. That's stupid."
7. _____ "I'm interested in hearing more."
8. _____ "Mmm." A sound that is neither positive nor negative.
9. _____ "What made you do something like that?"
10. _____ "Please continue. I'd like to hear more."
11. _____ The listener nods his or her head.
12. _____ "Oh, just forget it. It'll get better someday."
13. _____ "You're making a big problem out of nothing. It doesn't really matter."
14. _____ The listener looks into the speaker's eyes.

Reading at Work

Understanding New Words

(expanding vocabulary)

Read the sentences below. Find and circle the underlined words in the reading that follows.

1. For many diseases, <u>prevention</u> is easier than finding a cure. Sometimes a shot is all it takes to keep someone from getting a disease.

2. A discount is a price <u>reduction</u> or lowering. Reduction also means to have fewer of something.

3. Some cars have <u>defective</u> parts. These are parts that were made incorrectly.

4. Take your umbrella as a <u>precaution</u> in case it rains today.

5. We need to <u>eliminate</u> or remove all sources of air pollution.

Many companies have suggestion programs to give employees the chance to communicate their ideas to the management. The following reading is an example of a suggestion program's guidelines.

SUGGESTION GUIDELINES

A good suggestion is an original idea that will benefit the company. You must write your suggestion on the suggestion form. Put the signed form in any suggestion box.

Some Areas for Your Suggestions

- Improvements in current methods or practices
- Ways to lower use of materials, labor, or supplies
- Ideas for increasing productivity or efficiency
- Prevention or reduction of defective work or mistakes
- Improvements in quality of products or services
- Improvements in working conditions
- Safety precautions to eliminate or reduce accidents
- Methods to eliminate unnecessary paperwork

Understanding the Reading
(checking literal and inferential comprehension)

With a partner, discuss the suggested areas for improvement. Think about your job. Make as many suggestions for each of the areas as you can. Discuss your suggestions with the whole class. For example, maybe you have an idea about how the company could use some material, or scrap, that is currently being thrown away. Or maybe you can think of a faster or more efficient way to do your job. What about accidents? Can you think of some ways to prevent them?

   Does your company have a suggestion program? If you don't know, who could you ask about it? Have you ever made a suggestion at work? What was your suggestion? What was the result?

Writing
(filling out a suggestion form)

Review the Reading at Work section. Write about one of the suggestions you and your partner discussed or write about another idea you had for work improvement. Use the following form to make your suggestion.

SUGGESTION PROGRAM			
Name (please print)	*Dept.*	*Shift*	*Employee #*

Current practice or situation: _____

_____

_____

_____

My suggestion:_____

_____

_____

_____

_____

How my suggestion will benefit the company:_____

_____

_____

_____

_____

Signature: _____   Date: _____

Listening
(listening for specific information)

This is an example of an organization chart for a manufacturing company. It shows the working relationships in the company. Organization charts also show the formal communication process.

With your partner, take a few minutes to study the chart. Notice which jobs are on the same line horizontally. Notice the reporting relationships between jobs. Some information is missing. Listen to the audiotape and fill in the missing information on the chart.

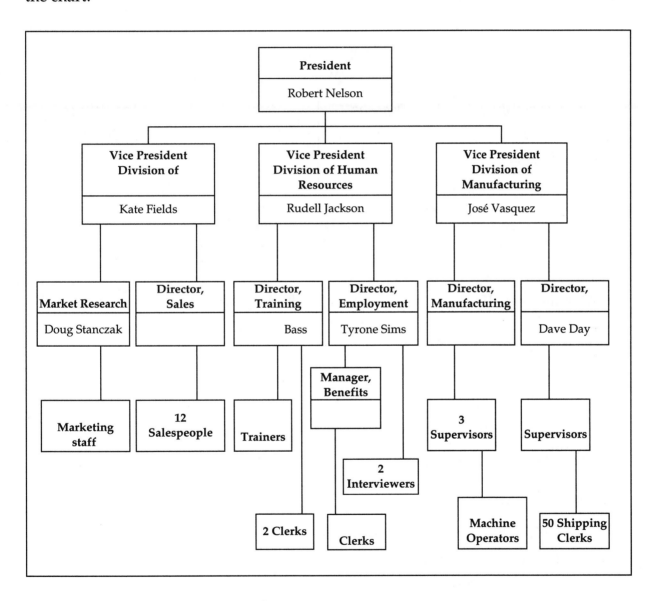

Using Math
(reconciling a bank account statement)

Every month your bank sends you a statement listing the deposits to and withdrawals from your checking account. When the statement comes, you should compare it to the entries in your checkbook. You want to make sure that both you and the bank agree about the amount of money in your account. This is called reconciling your bank account statement.

Several steps are necessary to reconcile your statement. Look at the information below and follow the steps.

FIRST FINANCIAL BANK
Statement from 07/25/92 through 08/24/92

Beginning Balance	Deposits	Checks	Ending Balance
07/25/92	amounts	amounts	08/24/92
$304.72	$447.13	$263.45	$488.40

Monthly service charge	Account number
$7.00	371 4859

From the checkbook:

A) Balance: $515.08

B) Deposits not on statement:
   1) $110.17
   2) 254.78
TOTAL_____

C) Checks not listed on statement:
   1) $ 50.00
   2)   27.50
   3) 210.10
   4)   43.67
TOTAL_____

To reconcile your statement:

1) Ending balance from the statement _____

2) Add the total deposits (B) _____

3)   SUB-TOTAL _____

4) Subtract the total checks (C) _____

5)   SUB-TOTAL _____

6) Subtract the service charge _____

7) Balance [should agree with (A)] _____

UNIT 6 Personalities and Conflicts

Before You Read
(*establishing prior knowledge, making predictions*)

Talk about the photograph with a partner.

Write your responses to the questions.

1. Who are these people? _____

2. What are they doing? _____

   _____

3. What do you think the problem is? _____

4. Do you think this is a good way to solve a problem at work?

   _____

   Why or why not? _____

   _____

Reading About Work

Labor Relations

"Hey, Wang, where are you?" Armando inquired jokingly.

"Oh, I'm sorry. Were you talking to me?" Wang asked. "I was just thinking about that union organizer we heard at lunch."

Wang and Armando were in the back seat of Kirk's car, riding home from work. Juanita was in the front, next to Kirk. The four had formed this car pool nearly three months ago.

"Kirk, what do you think about unions?" Wang asked.

"Well, that's a pretty broad question," Kirk replied. "Back in the '30s, workers' lives depended on the unions. Not only were workers exploited by getting low pay and working long hours, but there were serious health and safety hazards, as well. Individually, workers were powerless against their bosses. United, they made major changes in working conditions."

"But I don't see any of those problems, now," Armando said. "I think we're treated fairly at work."

"Maybe our company doesn't want us to unionize, so they are being very careful not to do anything to upset us," Juanita offered.

"Oh, I don't know about that, Juanita," Kirk said. "I've worked there for three-and-a-half years, and the supervisors have always been fair to me. Our salaries are good, and we get the same benefits as most of the people I know in other companies. Some of ours are even better. All in all, I'm pretty satisfied."

"Well, what about when they fired that woman last year for missing work when her child was sick? Did you think that was fair?" Armando asked Kirk.

"I don't know all the details, but I did hear she filed a grievance and got her job back after management reviewed the situation," Kirk answered.

"That's right," Juanita added. "Even without a union, we do have a grievance procedure, and there are laws that protect workers' rights. Many changes came about because of the unions."

"Oh, you mean like OSHA," Wang asked.

"Exactly," Kirk responded. "Between the unions and the laws, most companies that had unfair employment practices now have established procedures to ensure fair treatment. You know, things like the way we get to pick our vacations based on seniority. And how we are all allowed two warnings about being late before we can be fired."

"So, why would employees want a union if they are already getting fair treatment?" Wang persisted.

"Not everyone gets fair treatment, Wang," Juanita responded. "It depends on where you work. My girlfriend was just fired for not working overtime one day. She had no one to watch her children. Her supervisor told her that was her problem, not his. The company agreed with her supervisor, so now she has no job."

Kirk stopped the car. "Okay, Wang," Kirk said.

"What?" Wang asked, still deep in thought.

"Get out," Kirk said.

"Just because I asked so many questions? That's unfair! Is there a car pool union?" Wang asked.

When Wang realized he was home, he joined Kirk, Juanita and Armando in laughter.

"Can't you file a grievance like everyone else?."

Understanding New Words and Idioms

(expanding vocabulary)

A.   Work with a partner. Circle the word that best describes the word on the left as it was used in the reading. The first one is done as an example.

1. inquired   (asked)   answered

2. exploited   employed   used

3. offered   talked   suggested

4. persisted   continued   forgot

5. union   association   vegetable

6. organize   alphabetize   establish

7. grievance   complaint   recommendation

B.   With your partner, match the following terms to their definitions. Write the terms on the lines.

union organizer to unionize	individually to file a grievance	grievance procedure

1. _____ to form or join a labor union

2. _____ to express a formal, written complaint

3. _____ person who tries to get employees to join a union

4. _____ ordered series of steps taken to make a complaint about a situation at work

5. _____ by one's self

Understanding the Reading

(using words in context, checking literal comprehension)

Work with a partner. Fill in the blanks to complete the story. Your story should agree with the reading on pages 52–53.

Labor _____

Wang heard a _____ organizer speak at lunch. The organizer wanted

the _____ to join a labor union. Wang wanted to know more about

_____.

In the _____ on the way home, Wang asked his friends,

_____, _____, and _____, what they thought

about labor unions.

_____ told them that unions had helped workers in the 1930s

when workers were being _____. Back then, workers had received

_____ _____ for working _____ _____.

And the workers had serious _____ and _____ hazards where

they worked. The _____ got the employees to work together to make the

_____ change things.

Kirk and _____ talked about the woman who was _____

last year for missing _____ when her child was _____. Kirk

explained that the woman got her _____ back after she _____ a

_____ and _____ reviewed the situation.

_____ said not all _____ give their employees fair

_____. She told them about her _____ who was _____

because she couldn't work _____.

Discussing

Activity #1: Role play

(using spoken language, problem solving)

A flow chart shows the steps in a process and the order in which the steps occur. The flow chart on this page is typical of the steps in a grievance procedure for union employees. Read this chart with a partner, then do the role play.

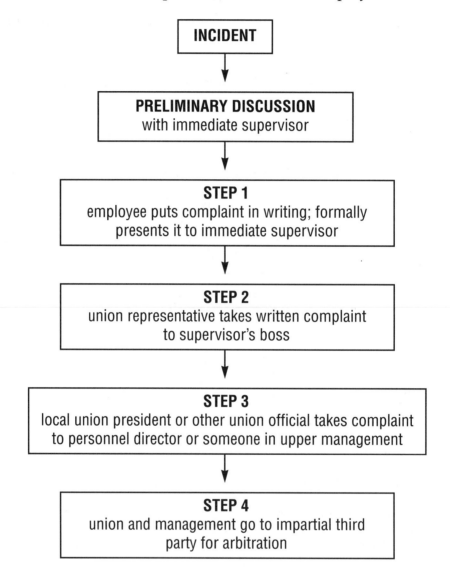

INCIDENT

↓

PRELIMINARY DISCUSSION
with immediate supervisor

↓

STEP 1
employee puts complaint in writing; formally presents it to immediate supervisor

↓

STEP 2
union representative takes written complaint to supervisor's boss

↓

STEP 3
local union president or other union official takes complaint to personnel director or someone in upper management

↓

STEP 4
union and management go to impartial third party for arbitration

Partner A is the employee. The incident is a change in the work schedule. The employee doesn't want to change his or her work schedule, but the employee's supervisor says that everyone must change work times and days off so that the company can increase production. The supervisor says the employee will be fired if he or she refuses to work the new hours and days. Partner B will play the role of the supervisor and the company's management and personnel representative in steps 2, 3, and 4. Partner A will play the role of the employee and then the union representative in steps 2, 3, and 4. The partners will present their arguments to the class. In the final step, the class will decide the outcome.

Activity #2 *(problem solving)*

A conflict arises between two people when each person tries to force his or her solution to a problem on the other person. Work with your partner to decide whether the suggestions below are things you should do or things you shouldn't do in conflict situations. Write *do* or *don't* on the line.

_____ 1. Be aware of the problem.

_____ 2. Understand the other person's point of view.

_____ 3. Ignore the problem.

_____ 4. Ask questions.

_____ 5. Say, "You're wrong, dead wrong!"

_____ 6. Keep a positive attitude.

_____ 7. Expect people to change their opinions and agree with you.

_____ 8. Ask the other person for suggestions.

_____ 9. Listen to the other person.

_____ 10. Look away.

_____ 11. Talk only about the things you disagree on.

_____ 12. Believe that you are always right.

_____ 13. Use humor when it fits the situation.

_____ 14. Say "I'd like to hear more of what you think about this problem."

_____ 15. Talk about areas in which you agree.

_____ 16. Focus on the problem and not on the personalities involved.

Writing
(clarifying problems, promoting effective communications)

When people are in a conflict situation, they sometimes lose their objectivity and say things that make the situation worse. One way of discussing the situation without allowing emotions to take over is through a method known as *I-messages*. Using this method, you clearly state what the problem is (without blaming the person), the way this situation makes you feel, and the concrete effects on you. For example, "Lois, when you are goofing off and not doing your work, I get upset because I know we'll all have to work late to make up for you." Think of some conflict situations at work and write *I-messages* that could help you.

State Problem	Your Feeling	Effect on You
"When . . .	I get (feel) . . .	because . . ."

Reading at Work

Understanding New Words

(expanding vocabulary)

Read the following sentences. With your partner, find and circle the underlined words in the reading.

1. Income maintenance means to keep someone's pay at the same level it has been in the past, even though there may be changes at work.

2. Severance pay is money a company pays an employee who has lost his or her job.

3. Seniority in a job means length of continuous service in that job.

4. A dispute is an argument.

5. A resolution is the solving of a problem.

The following is an example of some of the areas covered by union contracts with management.

Union–management contracts sometimes include:

- Wages and cost of living increases.
- Insurance and pension benefits.
- Income maintenance—a guarantee of minimum income or minimum work. Also severance pay benefits.
- Strikes and Lockouts—a union promises no strikes in return for management promising not to lock employees out of work during a labor dispute.
- Seniority clause—personnel decisions (promotions, layoffs, vacations, overtime, work schedules) are to be made on the basis of seniority.
- Dispute resolution—union–management disagreements follow specified procedures for resolution.

Understanding the Reading

(checking literal and inferential comprehension)

In a group of four, discuss the following questions about the reading.

1. Do union contracts usually specify a grievance procedure?
2. Is seniority important to union workers?
3. Do union employees usually get paid if the workload decreases?
4. Do union employees usually get paid if they lose their jobs?
5. Why would management want to lock the workers out of their workplace?
6. Why would employees want to strike?
7. What do you think is good about having a union contract?
8. What do you think is bad about having a union contract?

Listening
(understanding spoken language, problem solving)

Most companies have a list of policies and the disciplinary action that may be taken if a policy is violated. With your partner, read the following information. Discuss anything you don't understand.

A.   Policy violations for which an employee will be fired:

1. having firearms or other weapons at work

2. using or having drugs or alcohol at work

3. reporting to work while drunk or under the influence of drugs

4. hitting a supervisor or co-worker

5. stealing from the company or a co-worker

6. behaving indecently at work

7. forging or falsifying company documents

B.   Policy violations for which an employee may be fired, suspended, or receive a warning, depending on the situation:

8. using profane or abusive language

9. threatening a supervisor or co-worker

10. using a co-worker's ID card

11. punching a co-worker's time card

12. being absent or late many times

13. gambling at work

14. violating safety rules

15. refusing to do something your supervisor told you to do

Now listen to the conversations from the tape. Decide which policy applies to the situation and what the disciplinary action would be.

1. The policy that applies to this situation is number _____.

    The disciplinary action is _____

    _____.

2. The policy that applies to this situation is number _____.

    The disciplinary action is _____

    _____.

3. The policy that applies to this situation is number _____.

    The disciplinary action is _____

    _____.

4. The policy that applies to this situation is number _____.

    The disciplinary action is _____

    _____.

5. The policy that applies to this situation is number _____.

    The disciplinary action is _____

    _____.

Now listen as your partner reads a policy from page 60 out loud to you. You describe a situation that relates to the policy. Take turns reading a policy and describing the related situation. Use actual experiences from your job whenever you can.

Using Math and a Bar Graph

(calculating percentage increases, plotting a bar graph)

Assume that this 18-month contract will become effective on the first day of the month following the month we are currently in. We will call it *Day One* of the contract. (*Example:* If today is September 12, 1992, the contract will become effective October 1, 1992 and remain in effect until March 31, 1994.)

Using the following information, figure the increase in the hourly wage for a union employee. (If you need to review percentages, see Unit 4, Using Math, page 40.)

Current hourly wage: $6.75

Percent increase		Amount	New hourly wage
Day One	3.0%	_____	_____
6 months	1.5%	_____	_____
12 months	2.0%	_____	_____
18 months	4.0%	_____	_____

The standard workweek of 40 hours per week is equal to 2080 hours per year. To figure an annual salary, multiply 2080 by the hourly wage. Using the numbers from above, figure the new annual salary in each case.

Current annual salary   _____

After Day-One increase   _____

After 6-month increase   _____

After 12-month increase   _____

After 18-month increase   _____

Plot the annual salary increase on the bar graph. The current salary ($14,040) is done for you.

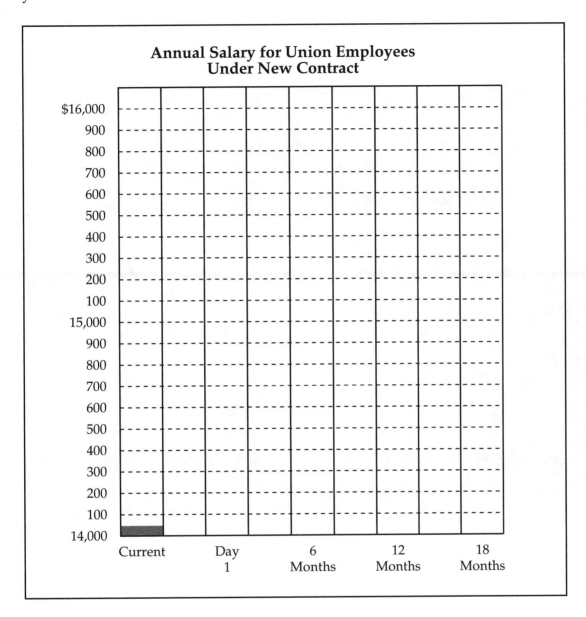

Before You Read
(establishing prior knowledge)

Discuss this photograph with a partner and answer the questions.

1. What is happening in this photograph? _____

2. Why? _____

3. Finish the sentence: "A good employee is . . ."_____

    _____

    _____

    _____

Reading About Work

Little Things Are Important, Too

Tyrone was walking through the building one day when he saw Ren picking up some paper from the floor. Ren put the paper in the wastebasket and continued on his way.

"Hi, Ren, what are you doing?" Tyrone asked. "Isn't this your break time?"

"Yes, it is, Tyrone," Ren answered. "I was on my way to the shop for a few supplies I need to finish the job I'm working on. I thought I would grab a cup of coffee while I was there."

"Do you mind if I tag along with you?" Tyrone inquired.

"Of course you can," Ren said, smiling. "After all, you're the boss!"

Tyrone laughed and said, "Ren, I want you to know how much I appreciate the work you do. You always volunteer for jobs. You do a good job. You never cut corners to make things easier. You always do extra things without complaining. Believe me, your actions do not go unnoticed."

"Thank you," Ren said. "But I just do my job. I'm not looking for special treatment or anything."

"I know that, Ren," Tyrone responded. "But I realize the self-discipline it takes to always do your best. And I am pleased with the initiative you show. You are always the first to offer constructive suggestions for improvements. You are a very valuable employee."

"It makes me feel good to hear you say these things, Tyrone," Ren began. "But you're the Manager of Maintenance for three big buildings. How do you know so much about what I do?"

"Oh, I get around," Tyrone said with a smile. "For example, I know that when you see paper on the floor, you pick it up, even though it isn't your job to do that kind of work. Little things are important, too, Ren. You show that you understand that."

Ren looked surprised. "I guess you do see a lot, Tyrone. I didn't know you saw me pick up paper!"

"That's the point, Ren," Tyrone said. "You do something because it needs to be done, not because you expect a reward. And you do it without being told. That's initiative. You're someone with a real future in this company."

"That's great!" Ren said. Then he laughed. "I just hope I don't get so busy watching for you now, that I forget to do my job," he joked.

Understanding New Words and Idioms

(using and expanding vocabulary)

Read the sentences with a partner. Circle the letter of the sentence that means the same as the numbered sentence.

1.   Tyrone <u>appreciates</u> Ren's work.

   a. Tyrone knows how good Ren's work is.

   b. Tyrone doesn't understand what Ren does at work.

2.   Ren has the <u>self-discipline</u> always to do his best.

   a. Ren's father checks Ren's work to see if it is good.

   b. Ren has trained himself to do good work every day.

3.   Ren has <u>initiative.</u>

   a. Ren is always willing and able to get things started.

   b. Ren watches someone else start new duties or projects.

4.   Ren offers <u>constructive suggestions</u> for improvements.

   a. Ren thinks of ways to make things better at work.

   b. Ren complains about things at work.

5.   Tyrone wanted to <u>tag along</u> with Ren to the shop.

   a. Tyrone wanted to see if he could get to the shop before Ren got there.

   b. Tyrone wanted to walk to the shop with Ren.

6.   Ren doesn't <u>cut corners</u> on his job.

   a. Ren does a complete job. He doesn't try to finish faster by leaving out some steps in the job.

   b. Ren walks down the middle of the hallway at work.

Understanding the Reading

(checking literal comprehension)

Read the statements with your partner. Circle *T* if the statement is true and *F* if the statement is false.

1. Tyrone is Ren's boss.	*T*	*F*
2. Ren is a good employee.	*T*	*F*
3. Tyrone thinks Ren wants special treatment.	*T*	*F*
4. Ren has good self-discipline.	*T*	*F*
5. Ren doesn't have any initiative.	*T*	*F*
6. Tyrone doesn't notice Ren's good work.	*T*	*F*
7. Ren likes to cut corners.	*T*	*F*
8. Ren has a good future where he works.	*T*	*F*

There are four false statements. Change the words to make true sentences. Write the new sentences on the lines below.

1. _____

2. _____

3. _____

4. _____

Discussing
(problem solving, role playing)

A. *Role Play:* Partners A and B are co-workers in the same department. The employees are being trained on a new piece of equipment. The equipment will not be installed for at least a month. Partner A is eager to try the new equipment in the training session. B thinks it isn't necessary to learn something they won't use for a month anyway. Talk about what A and B would say to each other.

B. *Rank Order:* With your partner, look at these reasons people work. Number them to show their order of importance to you and to your partner.

Reasons People Work	Myself	Partner
Provide for my family	_____	_____
Save money for the future	_____	_____
Learn new skills	_____	_____
Feel good about myself	_____	_____
Become a boss	_____	_____
Make lots of money	_____	_____
Make money for the company	_____	_____

Discuss your choices with the class. What other reasons can you think of why people work?

Writing
(critical thinking, using written language)

Write about a time at work when your actions showed one or more of the following:

self-discipline	initiative	constructive suggestions

Examples:

I used *self-discipline* when I worked very hard on a difficult project even though I knew no one could see me if I took it easy.

I made a *constructive suggestion* when we were behind in production and I thought of a faster way to pack the boxes.

I showed *initiative* _____

_____

I _____

_____

_____

_____

_____

_____

_____

_____

_____

_____

_____

_____

Reading At Work

Understanding New Words

(expanding vocabulary)

1. <u>Success</u> is the favorable result of someone's efforts.

2. A cause leading to a result is a <u>factor</u>.

3. A <u>motivated</u> person is excited about doing a good job or learning new things.

4. A person's <u>outlook</u> is how that person looks at life.

Some companies have posters like this one.

Understanding the Reading

(checking literal comprehension)

Discuss the reading with a small group of students. Answer the following questions.

1. Is a successful person usually happy?

2. If you think money is a success factor, how much money makes someone successful?

3. Think of someone who is a success. What makes that person successful?

4. Are you successful? Why or why not?

Listening
(understanding spoken language, using critical thinking)

The following words describe valued work behaviors. In a small group, discuss the words and meanings. Then listen to the situations on the audiotape. In the boxes following the words, write the word or words that describe the behavior in each situation.

showing initiative	acting motivated	accepting criticism
showing self-discipline	being dependable	being thorough

Situation 1	**Situation 2**
Situation 3	**Situation 4**

With your partner, take turns describing situations that show examples of the work behaviors listed above. Listen to each other carefully, so you can guess which behavior is being described. You may use examples of other valued work behaviors, too.

Using Math and a Line Graph

(reading a line graph, finding percentages)

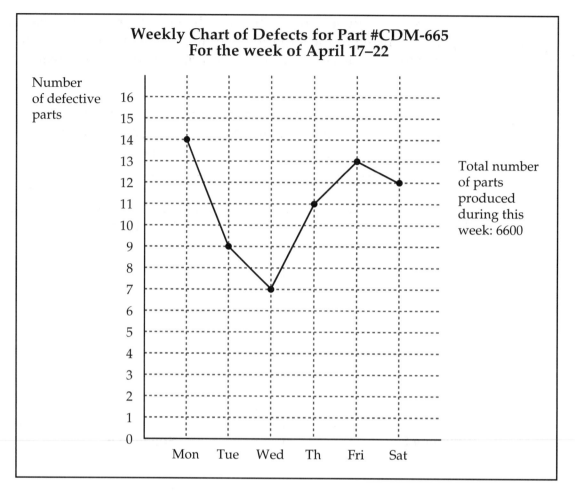

Weekly Chart of Defects for Part #CDM-665
For the week of April 17–22

Number of defective parts

Total number of parts produced during this week: 6600

1.   What information does this graph show? _____

_____

2.   How many defective parts were made each day during the week

of April 17–22?   Monday _____   Thursday _____

Tuesday _____   Friday _____

Wednesday _____   Saturday _____

3.   What is the total of defective parts for the week? _____

4.   How many parts were produced during this week? _____

5.   Find the percentage of defective parts produced. _____

Use this formula: $\dfrac{\text{Defective Parts}}{\text{Parts Produced}} \times 100 = \%\ \text{defective}$

(Defective Parts divided by Parts Produced multiplied by 100.)

UNIT 8 *Job Performance*

Talk about the photographs with a partner. Write your responses to the questions.

1. What kind of a business is this? _____

2. What is this company's attitude about quality? _____

   _____

3. Does anyone ever talk about quality where you work? _____

   Who? _____

   What does that person say about quality? _____

   _____

Reading About Work

The Business of Quality

It was very crowded in the small cafeteria. Usually the two hundred employees were working by 9 A.M., but this morning was different.

"So, what do you think this is all about?" Josephina asked Abdul.

"I think it's something about improving the quality of our work," Abdul said. "I heard that the company president is going to tell us about a program for quality improvement. I think it will affect our job-performance evaluations, too."

Just then Mr. Jackson, the company president, walked into the room.

"Good morning, hard-working employees," Mr. Jackson began. "I am very happy to see you all this morning. First, I want to thank you for the excellent work you have done this past year. Our profits have increased. Our customers have been very pleased with our products and quick delivery."

Mr. Jackson paused while the employees smiled proudly. Abdul and Josephina gave each other compliments on doing a good job. Other employees applauded.

"Because the company is doing so well," Mr. Jackson continued, "we will be able to give bigger salary increases on your performance evaluation this year. The increases will be between four and ten percent. The amount you receive will show how well you worked."

This time, all the employees applauded. Some yelled "Hooray!"

"One more thing," Mr. Jackson called out, "and then you can get back to your jobs." The employees became quiet.

Mr. Jackson looked into the employees' faces. "The focus for this year is quality," he said. "We are beginning a quality-improvement program and each of you will go to training classes. We want you to understand that our customers are not only the people who buy our products in the store. Each department you work with in this company is your customer, too. Treat each other as customers and do the best work you can. Then next year, we can give even bigger salary increases! Now, back to work."

"Remember, Josephina, as your customer, I am always right!" Abdul joked.

Abdul and Josephina laughed as they walked back to their departments.

Understanding New Words

(expanding vocabulary)

Match the word or words on the left with the words on the right.

1. job–performance evaluation
2. compliments
3. applauded
4. focus
5. quality

a. expressed approval by hitting the hands together

b. degree of excellence

c. expressions of praise, respect

d. central point of attention

e. supervisor's written opinion of how well an employee does his or her job

Understanding the Reading

(checking literal comprehension)

Answer the questions about the story. Use short answers.

1. Was the cafeteria crowded?

   Yes, it was. _____

2. Is Mr. Jackson the company president?

   _____

3. Is Mr. Jackson unhappy with the employees' work?

   _____

4. Will the employees get smaller salary increases this year?

   _____

5. Will the salary increases be between four and ten percent?

   _____

6. Are the employees happy about the salary increases?

   _____

7. Does the company have a new quality-improvement program?

   _____

8. Do Abdul and Josephina work in the same department?

   _____

Discussing

Activity #1: Role play *(using spoken language, critical thinking)*

Work with a partner. Partner A is from the Customer Relations Department of your company. Partner B wants to be a customer. Partner B wants to know how the company controls the quality of its products or services. Partner A describes the quality-control process. Also discuss management's policy and employees' attitudes about quality.

Activity #2 *(problem solving)*

Work with your partner. Think of at least four situations in which you did not receive quality service or products. (For example, you paid $30 for a pair of jeans. The first time you washed them, they fell apart because they were poorly made. Or, you received rude treatment from the employees in a restaurant or store.) Share your examples with the class. Discuss how these experiences make you feel about being a customer at that store or restaurant again.

Work in a small group. Select one of the situations discussed by the class. Your group is responsible for quality control at the place of business you selected. What will you do to make sure the customers have a good experience? *(Example:* Train employees with role-play situations on how to handle a rude customer by responding in a professional, courteous manner.)

Writing

(using written language, problem-solving)

Write about the quality-control plan you discussed in either Activity 1 or Activity 2 of the Discussing section of this chapter.

Type of workplace: (store, restaurant, factory, hospital, and so on) _____

_____

What kind of problem or problems are the result of poor quality control in this place

of business? _____

_____

_____

_____

_____

Describe a quality control program that will solve one of the problems stated above.

_____

_____

_____

_____

_____

_____

_____

_____

_____

_____

_____

_____

Reading at Work

Understanding New Words

(expanding vocabulary)

Read the sentences. Circle the underlined words in the reading.

1. A company's <u>reputation</u> is the opinion people have about that company's products and services.

2. A company <u>committed</u> to quality is a company that promises to make products without defects.

3. <u>Competitively priced</u> products are products that cost about the same as similar products.

4. When you are pleased with your work, you have a feeling of <u>satisfaction</u>.

This is an example of a company's statement of quality control.

"DO IT RIGHT THE FIRST TIME"

That's our idea of quality control. When you do it right the first time, you save time, money, and our reputation. This company is committed to delivering our products on time, competitively priced, and without defects. And quality starts with you—the employee. Think of your customers within the company. Those are the employees who receive your work. And think of our customers outside of the company. Those are the people who buy our products and services. Think of the enjoyment and satisfaction you will feel when you . . .

DO IT RIGHT THE FIRST TIME!

Understanding the Reading

(checking literal comprehension)

Work in a small group. Discuss your answers to the questions about the reading.

1. How does it save time, money, and the company's reputation to "do it right the first time"?

2. Do you agree that quality starts with the employee? Why or why not?

3. Who are your customers in your job? Do you have customers inside and outside of the company?

4. How do you usually feel about the quality of your work?

5. Does your company have a statement of quality? What is it?

Listening

(understanding spoken language, numbers)

A. Many employees have to record their production on charts such as the one on this page. On the audiotape, you will hear a new employee receive instructions about filling out this form. Listen to the tape. Fill out the chart with the information that the supervisor gives to the new employee.

DATA SHEET	Part No. _____				
Machine No.	Operator No. _____				
Pcs. per Hr.					
Date	Reasons for Reject				
Shift	Number Produced				Remarks/Corrective Action
First — 8:00 AM					
9:00 AM					
10:00 AM					
11:00 AM					
12:00 AM					
1:00 PM					
2:00 PM					
3:00 PM					

B. Work with a partner. You are going to fill out the chart for the second shift. Make up information that is similar to what you heard on the tape. One of you will give information for 4:00 P.M. through 7:00 P.M. The other will give information for 8:00 P.M. through 11:00 P.M. Take turns listening to your partner and filling out the chart. Check each other's charts for correct information.

Shift						
Second — 4:00 PM					
5:00 PM					
6:00 PM					
7:00 PM					
8:00 PM					
9:00 PM					
10:00 PM					
11:00 PM					

Using Graphs
(analyzing information from a line graph)

Many manufacturing companies use a quality control system called *Statistical Process Control* (SPC). This system uses a computer to plot statistical information (numbers) on a graph. The line formed by the numbers tells whether the parts being made are following company standards for quality.

Look at the following graph.

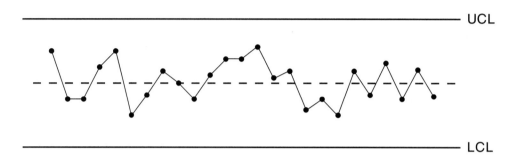

The solid line at the top is the Upper Control Limit (UCL). The solid line at the bottom is the Lower Control Limit (LCL). The points represent individual parts that were measured for certain information. The line connecting the points stays inside of the UCL and LCL. This means that the parts being made on this machine at this time are within the quality limits set by the company. This is called a "process in control."

Read the following graph and answer the questions.

PERCENT DEFECTS
Machine # __137__ Part # __7758639__
Date __06-10-92__ Pieces per hour __350__

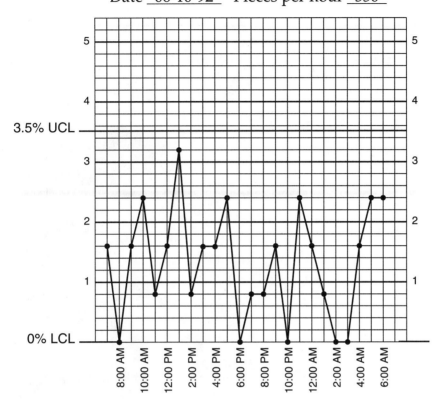

1. What information does this graph show? _____

_____

2. How many pieces per hour does this machine make? _____

3. What information is displayed vertically (up and down) on the graph?

_____

4. What information is displayed horizontally (left to right) along the top of

this graph? _____

What information is along the bottom? _____

5. What are the upper and lower control limits?

UCL _____ LCL _____

6. Is this process in control or out of control? _____

UNIT 9 *Goal Setting*

Before You Read
(establishing prior knowledge, predicting outcomes)

Look at the picture with a partner.

Answer the questions.

1. Where is the person in the picture? _____

2. What is she doing? _____

3. What goal do you think is in this person's future?

    _____

Reading About Work

Go for the Goal

The bell that began break time was very loud—loud enough that the employees could hear it over the noise of the machines. During break, however, the factory became quiet. The machines were shut down while the employees relaxed.

On the way to the employee lounge for break, Juana saw Bruno.

"Hi, Bruno," Juana said. "Could I talk to you for a minute?"

"Sure, Juana," Bruno replied. "What's on your mind?"

"I would like to become a supervisor," Juana began. "But I'm not sure what I need to do to get promoted. I thought you could give me some advice. You were promoted to supervisor eight months ago. How did you do it?"

"I set a goal for myself just as you have, Juana," Bruno began. "And then I developed a plan for reaching my goal."

Bruno and Juana entered the lounge and poured some coffee for themselves. Then they sat at the nearest table.

"How do I make a plan?" Juana asked.

"Think about what you need to achieve your goal," Bruno said. "Do you need more education or special training?"

"Well, I'll need good English for communicating with the employees, the managers, and other supervisors," Juana said. She was making notes on a piece of paper as they talked. "I'll need good math for doing the quality-control measurements of our products. And I'll need to learn about the company policies and forms that are the supervisor's responsibility."

"That's the idea," Bruno said. "Now you can make your plan. Your plan is a step-by-step guide that leads you to your goal."

"For example, I can go to night classes to learn more math and English," Juana said.

"That's one way," Bruno responded. "But to learn about company policies and forms, you'll need OJT."

"OJT?" Juana asked.

"On-the-job training," Bruno explained. "Your supervisor, Piotr, can recommend you for the company training program. Talk to him about your work. If you let him know your goal and your plan, he'll see you're serious about becoming a supervisor."

When the warning bell rang, it startled Juana because she was concentrating on her notes.

"I'll have to write out my plan after work," Juana said. "But thanks for the help you've given me."

"Glad to do it," Bruno said. "Come on, I'll walk back with you. I want to make sure I'm not standing near that bell when it rings the back-to-work signal!"

Understanding New Words and Idioms

(expanding vocabulary, using words in context)

Read the sentences with a partner. Decide together whether the meaning of the sentences is the same or different. Circle *Same* or *Different.*

1. Juana wanted Bruno's *advice* about about how she could get promoted.
    Juana wanted Bruno's recommendations for what she could do to get promoted.   *same*   *different*

2. Bruno told Juana how to *achieve* her goal.
    Bruno told Juana how difficult it would be for her to get promoted.   *same*   *different*

3. Bruno said she would need some *on-the-job training*.
    Bruno told Juana she would need to learn things specific to the company.   *same*   *different*

4. Juana was *startled* by the warning bell.
    Juana was afraid of the warning bell.   *same*   *different*

Read the sentence. Decide whether *a, b,* or *c,* has the same meaning. Circle *a, b,* or *c.*

"What's on your mind?" Bruno asked Juana.

a. Bruno wanted to know something about Juana's personality.

b. Bruno wanted to know what Juana was thinking.

c. Bruno wanted to know how intelligent Juana was.

Understanding the Reading

(checking literal comprehension, using critical thinking)

Read the sentences with a partner. Decide together whether the sentences are fact or opinion according to the story. Circle *fact* or *opinion.*

1. Juana wants to be a supervisor.   *fact*   *opinion*

2. Juana asks Bruno's advice about getting promoted.   *fact*   *opinion*

3. Bruno has the best information about getting promoted.   *fact*   *opinion*

4. Juana must go to night school to get promoted.   *fact*   *opinion*

5. On-the-job training is the only way to learn certain information.   *fact*   *opinion*

6. To get a promotion, you must have a written plan.   *fact*   *opinion*

Discussing

Activity #1: Role play *(critical thinking, problem solving)*

Many employees have a goal of being promoted or transferred to a different job. Plans for achieving this goal may vary but will usually include an interview for the new job.

With your partner, decide on a job at your workplace with which you are both familiar. Partner A will be the applicant (the employee applying for the job). Partner B will be the supervisor interviewing the applicant. Use the following questions for the interview. Also, write five more questions that are specific to the job. For example, for a supervisor's job you might ask, "What would you do if five people on your crew were absent one day?" Or if it's something the applicant has never done, ask, "Why do you think you would like doing machine set-ups?" The applicant can answer by talking about related abilities and interests.

1. What is your experience? Education?

2. What did you like most about other jobs you had? Least?

3. How do you get along with co-workers? Bosses?

4. What would you do if you didn't understand a part of your job?

5. What would you do if you made a mistake on your job?

6. What are your immediate goals? Future goals?

7. What is important to know about you?

8. Why should we promote (or transfer) you?

Activity #2: Short-term and long-term goals *(using critical thinking skills)*

In the reading, Juana's plan to achieve her goal was a list of immediate (short-term) goals that would lead to her future (long-term) goal.

With your partner, look at the groups of goals listed below and decide which are short- and which are long-term goals. On the line, write *S* for *short-term* or *L* for *long-term.*

_____ 1. Read employment ads in the newspaper.

_____ 2. Get a new job.

_____ 3. Ask friends if they know of any jobs available.

_____ 4. Put in applications at places I would like to work.

_____ 1. Save as much money as possible.

_____ 2. Ask friends and family if they know of houses for sale.

_____ 3. Buy a house.

_____ 4. Read the real estate ads in the newspaper.

_____ 1. Get brochures and catalogs for schools.

_____ 2. Save money.

_____ 3. Find out about financial aid programs.

_____ 4. Get a college degree or trade school certificate.

_____ 5. Ask friends what they know about the schools you are interested in.

Writing
(using written language, critical thinking)

Write about your goal or goals. Use the questions to guide you. Some examples are given.

- Long-term goal or goals: What do I want to do, to be, or to have one year (2 years, 5 years) from now?

- Short-term goal or goals: What do I need to do now to achieve my long-term goal?

- What do I have (or what actions have I taken) toward my goal?

- What problems may come up? (Such as, not having enough money.)

- What can I do to solve these problems? (Maybe get a loan.)

- If I need to sacrifice something (such as, not spending money on entertainment or a vacation), am I willing to do this?

- How much time will it take for me to achieve my short-term goal or goals? My long-term goal or goals?

GOAL PLANNING

Long-term goal_____

Short-term goal(s) _____

_____

I have _____

I need _____

Problems_____

Solutions_____

Sacrifices _____

   Okay or not okay? _____

Time frame—short-term goal_____

       long-term goal_____

Reading at Work

Understanding New Words

(expanding vocabulary)

1. Societies have standards for personal privacy. To wear clothing that goes against these standards is considered <u>indecent</u>.
2. Personal <u>hygiene</u> practices include routine bathing and hair washing and the use of deodorants and mouth cleaners.
3. <u>Relevant</u> questions are those directly related to the subject being discussed.

This is a useful guideline for going on an interview.

THE INTERVIEW: THINGS YOU SHOULD DO

1. Always be on time.

2. Wear clothes that fit comfortably and are in good condition. DO NOT wear indecent clothing.

3. Don't forget personal hygiene. Remember, your looks tell about you before you begin to speak.

4. Be relaxed, not shy. Give the interviewer a firm handshake. Keep good eye contact.

5. Always answer a direct question with the truth, even if you think it might hurt your chances for the job.

6. Be a good listener. Then show the interviewer how intelligent you are by asking relevant questions about the job.

Understanding the Reading

(using critical thinking, using spoken language)

Discuss these questions about the reading in a small group.

1. Why is it important to be on time to an interview?

2. Why is an applicant's appearance so important?

3. Should an applicant offer to shake hands or wait until the interviewer offers?

4. If you were in some legal trouble as a youngster, should you mention it to the interviewer before you are asked? Why or why not? If you are asked about it, what should you say?

5. How can the questions you ask show the interviewer how intelligent you are?

Listening
(understanding spoken language)

Interviewers often use charts like the one below to record applicants' responses to questions. On the audiotape, you will hear 3 applicants respond to different questions. Judging by the responses, decide which question is being answered by each applicant. In the appropriate box, make a note of a few words from the applicant's response.

	APPLICANTS		
	Dagmar	*Luigi*	*Carmen*
QUESTIONS 1. How would you increase production if your employees weren't meeting the required number of units per shift?			
2. It has always been a problem getting supplies from the warehouse when we need them. How would you fix this?			
3. What would you do if one employee repeatedly underperformed and got angry every time you talked to him or her?			

Review your completed chart with a partner. Take turns summarizing the applicants' responses. Check to see whether you and your partner agree on the responses.

Using Math
(understanding fractions)

A fraction represents part of a whole amount. The top number *(numerator)* shows a part of the whole amount. The bottom number *(denominator)* shows how many parts the whole amount is divided into. For example, $\frac{1}{2}$ is one part of a whole amount that has been divided into two parts.

Look at the ruler in the picture. How many parts is each inch divided into? _____ That number is the denominator. The arrow in the picture indicates a numerator of a fraction. What is the fraction? _____

1 inch   2 inches   3

Comparing Fractions

If the same number is used for both the numerator and denominator, the fraction is equal to 1. *Example:* $\frac{2}{2}$ = 1, $\frac{3}{3}$ = 1, and $\frac{16}{16}$ = 1. Only fractions with the same denominator can be compared with each other. To determine which fraction is larger, compare which has the larger numerator. *Example:* $\frac{5}{8}$ is larger than $\frac{3}{8}$.

Circle the larger fraction in these pairs: $\frac{3}{16}$ $\frac{7}{16}$, $\frac{5}{8}$ $\frac{6}{8}$, $\frac{3}{4}$ $\frac{2}{4}$, $\frac{2}{6}$ $\frac{5}{6}$, $\frac{7}{12}$ $\frac{6}{12}$.

To compare fractions with different denominators, find a common denominator. A *common denominator* is a number that the fractions being compared will go into evenly. *Example:* You want to compare $\frac{6}{16}$ and $\frac{14}{32}$ to see which number is larger. The denominators are 16 and 32. Both these numbers can be divided evenly into 32: 16 goes into 32 twice, so multiply the fraction $\frac{6}{16} \times \frac{2}{2} = \frac{12}{32}$.

Now compare $\frac{12}{32}$ to $\frac{14}{32}$. The fraction with the larger numerator is larger.

Convert the following fractions by finding the common denominator. Then write the larger fraction on the line. If the fractions are equal, write *equal* on the line.

_____ 1. $\frac{1}{4}$ $\frac{4}{16}$

_____ 2. $\frac{6}{8}$ $\frac{3}{4}$

_____ 3. $\frac{7}{16}$ $\frac{4}{32}$

_____ 4. $\frac{8}{64}$ $\frac{5}{8}$

_____ 5. $\frac{12}{16}$ $\frac{1}{2}$

_____ 6. $\frac{3}{8}$ $\frac{2}{32}$

_____ 7. $\frac{2}{2}$ $\frac{4}{4}$

_____ 8. $\frac{7}{64}$ $\frac{5}{32}$

_____ 9. $\frac{30}{32}$ $\frac{50}{64}$

_____ 10. $\frac{32}{64}$ $\frac{16}{32}$

UNIT 10 *Job Training and Continuing Education*

Before You Read
(establishing prior knowledge, making predictions)

Look at the photograph.

Discuss these questions with your partner.

Write your answers to the questions on the lines.

1. Where are these people? _____

2. Why are they here? _____

3. Do you think what they are doing is important? _____

   Why or why not?_____

Reading About Work

You're Never Too Old to Learn Something New

On Tuesday after work, the members of the car pool were riding silently. It had been busy at work lately and everybody was tired on the ride home.

"I won't be riding home with you on Friday," Ramona announced. "I have an appointment with a counselor at the community college."

"Oh," Waclaw said, "are you thinking about taking some classes?"

"Well, I would like to be a medical assistant," Ramona said. "But I don't know whether my English is good enough to take the classes I need. The counselor is going to talk to me and maybe give me some tests."

"I think that's great!" Erico said. "I've been thinking about taking some classes to study for my GED. Could I go with you on Friday to pick up some information?"

"Sure," Ramona answered.

"What's GED?" Lina asked.

"GED stands for General Educational Development," Erico responded. "It's a certificate of achievement for people who didn't finish high school."

"I'd like to get a college degree," Lina said. "But I'm afraid my English isn't good enough to read the college textbooks."

"I'm studying English now. I take ESL classes at the college," Waclaw said. "I started in the beginning level last year. You can learn a lot and have fun, too."

"Maybe I'm too old to learn," Lina said. "And maybe it's not important for me to get a college degree. After all, I already have a job."

"What if something happens to your job, or maybe you'll want to try for a better job someday," Ramona said. "You are never too old to learn something new."

"I'm still a little nervous about studying. After all, it has been a long time since I was in school," Lina said.

"Isn't there something you could take to sort of ease your way back into the routine?" Waclaw asked. "You know, something you would enjoy knowing more about, but not a class where you would have too much homework."

"Well, I've always been interested in photography," Lina replied. "Do they have classes like that?"

"Sure," Ramona said. "And if we register for classes that meet at the same time, then we can car pool to school together, too."

"Oh, I'm going to miss these conversations in the car," Erico said.

"Miss them? We're still going to be together every day in the car," Waclaw said.

"Yes, but we'll all be too busy thinking about what we're learning to talk to each other!" Erico said with a laugh.

Understanding New Words

(expanding vocabulary)

Read the sentences below. With a partner, decide whether *a* or *b* has the same meaning as the numbered sentence. Circle letter *a* or *b*.

1. She wants to be a <u>medical assistant</u>.

    a. She wants to work as a helper to doctors and nurses.

    b. She wants to be a nurse.

2. On Thursday you can <u>register</u> for classes at the community college.

    a. On Thursday you can go to classes at the community college.

    b. On Thursday you can fill out the forms to take classes at the community college.

3. The president <u>announced</u> the names of the people who completed the classes.

    a. The president called out the names of the people who completed the class.

    b. The president whispered the names of the people who completed the class.

4. I want to study for the <u>GED</u> certificate.

    a. I want to study for the General Educational Development certificate.

    b. I want to study for the General Electricity Diploma certificate.

5. Good students are proud of their <u>achievement</u>.

    a. Good students are proud of the success they have.

    b. Good students are proud of their jobs.

6. A <u>counselor</u> is one of the best sources of advice to students about school and classes.

    a. A person who has special training and information is one of the best sources of advice to students about school and classes.

    b. Any person who speaks and reads English is one of the best sources of advice to students about school and classes.

Understanding the Reading

(checking literal comprehension)

A. The Main Idea: Read the sentences with a partner. Circle the letter of the sentence that gives the main idea of the reading.

    a. Everyone should go to school to learn English.

    b. Education is important for improving your life.

    c. Community colleges are not expensive.

    d. All people in car pools are friends.

B. Sequencing: Read the sentences. Write them in the order they occurred in the reading.

- On Friday, they will go to the college together.
- Waclaw told Lina he started studying English last year.
- Ramona said she plans to see a counselor at the community college on Friday.
- Lina decided to take some classes.
- On Tuesday, Ramona, Lina, Erico, and Waclaw rode home from work together.
- Erico said he wants to go to the college to register for GED classes.

_____

_____

_____

_____

_____

_____

WAISGLASS/COULTHART

"Milner, we finally found a job for you that doesn't require any computer training."

Discussing
(using spoken language, critical thinking)

Checklist of Reasons for Returning to School

Read the checklist that follows and with your partner, discuss the reasons for going back to school. Put a check (✔) in the proper column for things that apply to you and your partner. Write any reasons you or your partner think of that aren't on the list.

		Myself	Partner
1.	I need better English for everyday use.	____	____
2.	I want a better job.	____	____
3.	I want to help my children with schoolwork.	____	____
4.	I want to meet new people.	____	____
5.	I want to get a high school diploma or GED.	____	
6.	I want to get a college degree.	____	____
7.	I want to get a technical certificate.	____	____
8.	I want to pursue personal interests.	____	____
9.	_____	____	____

Now do the same for reasons why it is difficult to go to school.

Reasons Why It Is Difficult to Go to School

1.	I work long hours everyday.	____	____
2.	I don't have a car.	____	____
3.	It costs too much.	____	____
4.	I want to spend time with my family.	____	____
5.	I don't have a babysitter.	____	____
6.	The class schedule conflicts with my work schedule.	____	____
7.	I have too many responsibilities at home.	____	____
8.	_____	____	____

Problem solving: Working in a small group, use the list of reasons why it is difficult to go to school and suggest ways to solve those problems. For example, if the problem is "I work long hours everyday," one possible solution is "Take a class that meets only one time a week."

Reading at Work

Understanding New Words
(expanding vocabulary)

1. Courses that are <u>comparable</u> means the courses can be compared and found to be similar.
2. <u>Technology</u> courses are concerned with new developments in areas such as science, electronics, computers, and medicine.
3. <u>Leisure time</u> is time not dedicated to specific work or a job. Most people use their leisure time to relax, play sports or pursue other enjoyable activities.

This is an example of a page from a community college brochure.

Explore College

Community College—it's close to home, features outstanding educational opportunities, and saves you money.

- **Arts and Sciences**
  These courses are comparable to the freshman and sophomore requirements at four-year universities. Take those classes here and earn an associate's degree. Then, you can have your credits transferred to the college or university of your choice.

- **Health, Advanced Technology, and Business**
  These courses prepare you for tomorrow's technology in computer-aided design, data processing, nuclear medicine and many other fields.

- **Continuing Education Courses**
  People of all ages can broaden their experiences through creative use of leisure time. Learn how to reupholster your couch, fix home appliances, or pick up some phrases before your next trip to a foreign country.

- **Developmental Education Courses**
  Develop your reading, writing, mathematics, and study skills so you can realize your full potential in school—and life.

Understanding the Reading
(using critical thinking, using spoken language)

In a small group, discuss these questions.

1. What are some specific courses in the area of Arts and Sciences? Continuing Education? Developmental Education?
2. Have you ever taken any classes at a community college? What were they? Why did you take them? What did you think of them?

Listening

(understanding spoken language)

Listen to the tape recording of classes offered by a community college. Use the grid below to fill in the information about class offerings. Fill in the names of the classes in the area corresponding with the days and times the classes will be held.

Time	Mon. Med. Asst.	Mon. GED	Tues. Med. Asst.	Tues. GED	Wed. Med. Asst.	Wed. GED	Thurs. Med. Asst.	Thurs. GED	Fri. Med. Asst.	Fri. GED	Sat. Med. Asst.	Sat. GED
4:00p												
5:00p												
6:00p												
7:00p												
8:00p												
9:00p												
10:00p												

Follow-up Discussion: Ramona and Erico want to take classes at the same time. Ramona wants to take a class for Medical Assistants and Erico wants to study for his GED. On Monday and Wednesday, they work until 6:00 P.M. The rest of the week they work until 4:00 P.M. Circle the classes on the school schedule that would fit into Ramona's and Erico's schedules.

Writing
(using written language)

Some schools require students to give a writing sample at the time of registration. The writing sample helps the counselors and teachers decide which class is the right level for the student. The following is an example of the type of questions asked in writing samples.

Write a paragraph about why you want to go to school. What are your goals? What are your reasons for taking classes? What kinds of classes do you want to take? Why?

_____

_____

_____

_____

_____

_____

_____

_____

_____

_____

_____

_____

_____

_____

_____

_____

_____

_____

Using Math
(changing fractions to decimals)

If you are working with measurements that are in fractions, and you are using a calculator, you will have to change the fractions to decimals before you can enter the numbers into the calculator.

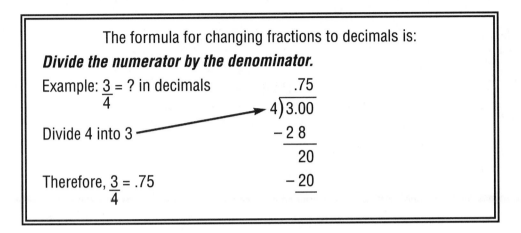

The formula for changing fractions to decimals is:

Divide the numerator by the denominator.

Example: $\frac{3}{4}$ = ? in decimals

Divide 4 into 3

Therefore, $\frac{3}{4}$ = .75

$$\begin{array}{r} .75 \\ 4\overline{)3.00} \\ -2\,8 \\ \hline 20 \\ -20 \\ \hline \end{array}$$

Change the following fractions to decimals

1. $\frac{5}{12}$ $\qquad$ $\frac{7}{8}$ $\qquad$ $\frac{5}{32}$ $\qquad$ $\frac{1}{2}$

2. $\frac{3}{20}$ $\qquad$ $\frac{4}{5}$ $\qquad$ $\frac{15}{16}$ $\qquad$ $\frac{13}{32}$

3. $\frac{7}{18}$ $\qquad$ $\frac{5}{7}$ $\qquad$ $\frac{4}{11}$ $\qquad$ $\frac{11}{15}$

4. $\frac{23}{32}$ $\qquad$ $\frac{9}{16}$ $\qquad$ $\frac{2}{3}$ $\qquad$ $\frac{5}{14}$

5. $\frac{1}{6}$ $\qquad$ $\frac{3}{32}$ $\qquad$ $\frac{5}{8}$ $\qquad$ $\frac{4}{9}$

6. $\frac{8}{13}$ $\qquad$ $\frac{3}{5}$ $\qquad$ $\frac{18}{19}$ $\qquad$ $\frac{3}{16}$

Audio Tape Scripts

Unit 1—Listening
Student Text Page 8

SECRETARY:	Hello. Good Health Insurance. How may we help you?
FRANCISCO:	Yes, I have some questions about a statement I received from your company. Who can I talk to?
SECRETARY:	That'll be Ms. Johnson. Hold on, please, while I transfer your call.
SFX:	CLICK, BUZZ
MS. JOHNSON:	Ms. Johnson. May I help you?
FRANCISCO:	Yes, I have some questions about a statement I received. My name is Francisco Lara and my social security number is 357-09-0245.
MS. JOHNSON:	Thank you Mr. Lara. What is you company's name?
FRANCISCO:	It's Robertson's Plastics.
MS. JOHNSON:	And the date and claim number on the statement you received?
FRANCISCO:	The date is July 7, 1993. The claim number is 025670B, as in "boy".
MS. JOHNSON:	Okay, I have it now. What can I help you with?
FRANCISCO:	Well, the first charge is $25.00 for a doctor visit on June 3, but the amount in the "total paid" column is only $15.00. Where's the other $10.00?
MS. JOHNSON:	Oh, there should be a $10.00 amount listed in the column marked "deductible".
FRANCISCO:	Oh, I see. And what about the next charge? It's for minor surgery on the same day. The charge was $40.00, and under the column marked "not covered" it says $40.00. Why is that?
MS. JOHNSON:	Oh, there's something left off your form. In the column for "Reason Code", it should say "MSY". It means your insurance doesn't pay for that kind of medical service.
FRANCISCO:	Well, that clears everything up. Thanks for your help. Good-bye, Ms. Johnson.
MS. JOHNSON:	Good-bye, Mr. Lara.

Unit 2—Listening
Student Text Page 18

ANNCR: Monday.

SUPERVISOR: When you leave the lab, turn left. Go through the hallway. Pass the elevators and the stairs. Enter the doorway straight ahead of you.

ANNCR: Where are you?

ANNCR: Tuesday.

SUPERVISOR: When you leave the lab, turn left and walk in the hallway until you get to the stairs. Take the stairs down one floor. On the 2nd floor, the stairs open into the unit.

ANNCR: Where are you?

ANNCR: Wednesday.

SUPERVISOR: Leave the lab, walking straight ahead until you get to the open hall on your right. Turn right. You will see an elevator ahead on your left. Take the elevator to the second floor. Exit the elevator and turn left. Go through the doorway.

ANNCR: Where are you?

ANNCR: Thursday.

SUPERVISOR: Leave the lab and walk forward to the open hall on your right. Turn right and walk to the elevator. Take the elevator all the way down to the first floor. When you leave the elevator, turn right. Walk straight ahead and go through the doorway.

ANNCR: Where are you?

ANNCR: Friday.

SUPERVISOR: Leave the lab. Go straight, then turn right and walk all the way through the open hallway. Just past the stairs and elevator, turn right. Continue straight ahead through the doorway.

ANNCR: Where are you?

(Approx. time: 1 minute, 15 seconds)

Unit 3—Listening
Activity #1—Student Text Page 28

(Time: 1 minute)

ANNCR: Recommendations for protective equipment and requirements for the safe use of Product HC-1357.

(Pause)

Eyes—Employees using this chemical are required to wear safety glasses.

(Pause)

Hands—Employees must wear gloves to prevent skin contact. Also, employees must wash hands before eating, even if gloves were used.

(Pause)

Skin—Regular clothing should prevent most skin contact. However, this clothing must be washed before being worn again.

(Pause)

Other—This product should be used where there is plenty of fresh air. If not, employees must be given special masks to aid breathing.

Activity #2—Student Text Page 28

(Time: 1 minute 25 seconds)

MR. JACKSON:	Hi, Betty. Thanks for coming by. I need to check the information on this employee injury report. By the way, are you okay now?
BETTY:	Sure, Mr. Jackson. Thanks for asking. So, what do you need to know?
MR. JACKSON:	Well, I thought your last name had an "e" on the end of it. Does it?
BETTY:	Yes, it's spelled "B - r - o - w - n - e." First name "B - e - t - t - y."
MR. JACKSON:	First name's okay. What's your employee number?
BETTY:	7 - 1 - 1 - 5 - 9 - 4.
MR. JACKSON:	Okay, I'll fix that. This part I know is correct. You are a housekeeper in the housekeeping department.
BETTY:	That's right.
MR. JACKSON:	Now, when did this accident happen?
BETTY:	It was last Tuesday, so that's December 9, 1992. And it was at the beginning of my shift—8 o'clock in the morning.
MR. JACKSON:	8 in the morning? And December 9th? Boy, this information is all messed up! So you were on duty, weren't you?
BETTY:	Yes, I was.
MR. JACKSON:	But it did happen in the Main Lobby, didn't it?
BETTY:	No, it was in the storage area on the 2nd floor.
MR. JACKSON:	Maybe you'd better describe the injury to me. I get the feeling I'll probably have to make some more corrections.
BETTY:	Well, I was emptying a wastebasket . . .
MR. JACKSON:	So far, so good . . .
BETTY:	When a piece of glass fell out and cut my left arm.
MR. JACKSON:	Hmph! (Sort of an "I knew it!" grunt.)
	(Under his breath he mutters "one, two, three . . ." as though counting mistakes on the paper.)
	Well, it's a good thing I always check the information on these reports. There were 8 mistakes on this form.

Unit 4—Listening
Student Text Page 38

(See photos on page 38–39)

Scenario 1

JOSE: Hi, you must be the new employee. I'm Jose.

ALFREDO: Nice to meet you. My name is Alfredo.

JOSE: So, Alfredo, I've been here almost three years now and I was just wondering — what do they pay for a starting salary these days?

Scenario 2

WOMAN 1:   What a beautiful new car and you got all the extras, too. That must really have been expensive!

WOMAN 2:   Oh, we saved for it for quite a while.

WOMAN 1:   Really? So how much was it?

Scenario 3

ALICIA: Someone told me that her parents send her money every month so she can dress like that.

TEDDY: Well, it sure can't be on her salary alone 'cause she and Karen, here, have the same job and even started at the same time, right, Karen?

KAREN: Well, yes, Teddy . . .

ALICIA: And you know you can't afford to dress like that! So, Karen, what do you figure her folks send her anyway? A couple hundred a month?

Scenario 4

MAN WITH ACCENT: I don't think it's our co-worker's or Management's business whether we speak English or our native language at work. As long as we get the job done, that's all that should matter to them.

Activity #2—Student Text Page 39

Messages

1. Roberto Carlucci's retirement party will be Friday, October 12 at the Pasta Villa Restaurant. Be there at 7 o'clock sharp, and don't forget the $25.50 donation.

2. The company's softball team needs 5 volunteers to sell refreshments during the games. You must be able to come every Tuesday and Thursday from 6 to 8 p.m. You will be responsible for serving 150 to 200 fans and players.

3. Two weeks from now, the Production Department is going to get a $.73 raise, and the Service Department is going to get a $.64 raise. All clerical employees will receive a 7 percent raise, but they won't get it for 3 to 6 months.

Unit 5—Listening
Student Text Page 49

MR. SIMS:	As the new Manager of Benefits, Ms. Gomez, you will need to familiarize yourself with the company. A good way to do that is to study this organization chart. t shows you the names and titles of most of the management and how many employees there are in each department.
MS. GOMEZ:	I see. But some of the information is hard to read, Mr. Sims. Could you help me out?
MR. SIMS:	Certainly. What do you need to know?
MS. GOMEZ:	Well, starting at the top, I know that Robert Nelson is the President, and Kate Fields, Rudell Jackson and Jose Vasquez are the Vice Presidents, but I can't read the name of Kate Fields' division.
MR. SIMS:	She is Vice President of Marketing and Sales.
MS. GOMEZ:	Okay. And reporting to her are Doug Stanzak, Director of Market Research and who is the Sales Director?
MR. SIMS:	That's Greg Chu, spelled C-h-u.
MS. GOMEZ:	Okay. And I see there are 12 salespeople and how many in marketing?
MR. SIMS:	There are 5 people on the marketing staff.
MS. GOMEZ:	Now, in the Human Resources Division, my name goes into the space for Manager of Benefits—Rosa Gomez. And I have 2 clerks reporting to me.
MR. SIMS:	That's right. And the Director of Training, Ray Bass, has just added another trainer, so that brings the total number of trainers to 3.
MS. GOMEZ:	Looks like that only leaves us with the Manufacturing division, Jose Vasquez, Vice President. Who reports to him?
MR. SIMS:	The Director of Manufacturing is Van Thieu, T-h-i-e-u, and the Director of Shipping is Dave Day. They each have 3 supervisors reporting to them.
MS. GOMEZ:	And there are 187 machine operators and 50 shipping clerks, right?
MR. SIMS:	That's correct. Now is your chart complete?
MS. GOMEZ:	It's complete, but I think I'm going to have to study it for a while to learn who's who!

Unit 6—Listening
Student Text Page 60

Conversation # 1

SUPERVISOR: Oh, Miguel, could I see you a minute?

EMPLOYEE: Yes, Mrs. Martinez. What is it?

SUPERVISOR: I was looking at this purchasing order and I noticed that my signature is on it, but I didn't sign this. Can you tell me anything about it?

EMPLOYEE: Well, I couldn't find you when I making the order that day, so I just put your name there. I know it is supposed to have your signature or they won't fill the order. I had to do it a couple times before.

SUPERVISOR: You've signed my name on company documents before this? Didn't you know you weren't supposed to do that?

EMPLOYEE: Yes, I knew. But I didn't think you would find out.

Conversation # 2

EMPLOYEE: Oh, Mr. Dixon, I'm sorry I'm late, but it's just...

SUPERVISOR: It's just the 12th time this month you've been late, Lester, and today is only the 25th. You've still got 4 working days left. What are you doing? Going for some kind of world record?

Conversation # 3

SUPERVISOR: Well, guys, what have you got to say for yourselves?

EMPLOYEE 1: It wasn't me. He started it. He's always mouthing off. This time he went too far.

EMPLOYEE 2: Me? You're the one who's such a hot head! Ask anyone in the department. You try to joke with this guy and have some fun and the next thing you know he's punching your lights out. I only fought back to protect myself.

Conversation # 4

SUPERVISOR: I'm sorry about this, but rules are rules.

EMPLOYEE: But I thought that since the office was getting all new furniture, the old stuff would just be thrown away.

SUPERVISOR: Why didn't you ask me about it? I could have told you that we had plans for it. It has hardly been used, you know that. For you to come back after the office is closed and try to sneak two chairs and a table out of here covered in sheets, I have to believe you knew you were doing something wrong.

Conversation # 5

SUPERVISOR: You know, we make these rules for your own protection. I realize it may take you a little longer to get dressed every day, but when you are assigned to work in the construction area, you must wear all the equipment that you've been given.

EMPLOYEE: I know. But I'm really on the edge of the area and I stay as far away from the machines as I can. I just didn't think it was all that necessary. Besides, it's so hot today, and all that protection just makes me hotter and more uncomfortable.

SUPERVISOR: I can understand your feelings about this, but the areas that require special precautions are clearly marked and you know where they are, don't you?

EMPLOYEE: Yes, I do. And I was working in a special precautions area.

Unit 7—Listening
Student Text Page 71

ANNCR: Situation 1

RHONDA: Come on, Eva. I've been standing all day. I want to go over there and sit down. No one will see us.

EVA: We have to do this work, Rhonda, Mr. Randolph told me to mark on this paper if there were any problems with the contents of these boxes. Let's get busy. There must be 50 boxes here.

RHONDA: Someone from Quality Control checks it after us, so let them find out if it's okay. At least the boxes will be checked before they leave the factory.

EVA: Not if people in Quality Control think like you do, Rhonda. They could think why should they bother to check them because we already checked them here. These boxes could get out without ever being checked by anyone. Besides, Mr. Randolph is depending on me.

RHONDA: Okay, I guess you're right.

ANNCR: Situation 2

RANDOLPH: Luis, what are you doing over there?

LUIS: Oh, hi, Mr. Randolph. I'm just checking the contents of these boxes. I want to be sure all the parts in here are okay.

RANDOLPH: But I didn't ask you to do that, Luis.

LUIS: I know. But it has to be done and I've already finished my work. I thought I might as well find something to do until it's time to go home.

ANNCR: Situation 3

CLARA: Come on, Suzette. Our break's over. I'll walk back to the department with you.

SUZETTE: Aw, cool your jets, Clara. We've got time. Miss Willis is at a staff meeting. She'll never know if we're late.

CLARA: I'm going back now, Suzette. I have work to do and I want to get it done. It really doesn't matter to me whether Miss Willis is watching or not. I really want to check over that report I typed.

SUZETTE: I thought you already checked it.

CLARA: I did, but I would like to check it again to be really sure everything is correct. See you later.

ANNCR: Situation 4

WILLIS: Suzette, could I speak with you, please?

SUZETTE: Yes, Miss Willis. What is it?

WILLIS: Suzette, you take too long on your breaks and you don't act very interested in your job. Is there a problem you want to talk about?

SUZETTE: No, Miss Willis. In fact, I have been thinking about my work behavior lately and I'm going to work on improving it.

WILLIS: That's good, Suzette. You know I like you, but you need to have a better attitude about your work or you won't last long here. Do you understand?

SUZETTE: Yes, Miss Willis, I understand. I'll do better. Thanks for giving me another chance.

Unit 8—Listening
Student Text Page 79

DEBBIE: Okay, Raji, let me show you how to fill out this chart. It is something you must do every day, but it's really pretty simple to learn.

RAJI: I'm ready. Tell me what to do.

DEBBIE: First, put down the number of the machine you worked on today.

RAJI: It was number 1351, wasn't it?

DEBBIE: That's right. And it is programmed for 150 pieces per hour.

RAJI: One-fifty, okay. And the date is 06-20, right?

DEBBIE: Correct. Now move to the top of the page where it says "Part Number". That was 266704.

RAJI: 266704. Got it. And my operator number is 0247.

DEBBIE: Good, Raji. You are understanding this quickly. The next thing to look at is "Reason for Reject". For this part there are three reasons: broken part, missing part and bad part. So under "reasons" you can write "broken", "missing", and "bad".

RAJI: Broken, missing, bad. What's next?

DEBBIE: Well, today, I kept a count of your hourly production. These numbers go next to the hour on the left side of the chart. 8:00 - 110 pieces. 9:00 - 105 pieces. 10:00 - 120 pieces. 11:00 - 100 pieces. 12:00 - 100 pieces. 1:00 - 106 pieces. 2:00 - 100 pieces. And 3:00 - 115 pieces. Did you get that?

RAJI: Well, let me check. Reading down the left column that is headed "Number Produced" I have 110, 105, 120, 100, 100, 106, 100, and 115. Is that right?

DEBBIE: Yes, it is. Now, let's do the reject count. At 8:00 you had 1 broken part. At 9:00, 1 broken part and 1 missing part. At 10:00, 2 missing parts and 1 bad part. At 11:00, 2 broken parts and 1 bad part. At 12:00, no defects. At 1:00, 1 bad part. At 2:00, 3 missing parts and 3:00, no defects. Do you have all that?

RAJI: I think so. Let me read it back to you. I will read down each column to check the numbers. Under "broken" I have 1, 1, none, and 2. The rest of the column is empty.

DEBBIE: Yes, that checks. How about "missing"?

RAJI: 8:00 AM none, then 1, 2, none, none, none, 3, then none at 3:00 PM. Right?

DEBBIE: Good. And for "bad parts"?

RAJI: None at 8:00 and 9:00. Then 1 at 10:00, 1 at 11:00 and the last 1 at 1:00 PM. No others. Is that right?

DEBBIE: That's right. Only one other thing left to put on the chart, Raji. Did you notice that you didn't produce the 150 pieces per hour that the machine is set up for?

RAJI: Yes, I wondered about that.

DEBBIE: Well, it's because you're new. So in the column headed "Remarks/Corrective Action" just put "new employee in training". Now, we're finished.

Unit 9—Listening
Student Text Page 89

INTERVIEWER: That's the situation, Carmen. What do you think?

CARMEN: Well, since you say this problem has a long history, first I would want to analyze the current delivery system and look at all the solutions that have been tried in the past. I would determine what was causing the delays now and see if I could work around it. Not knowing the answer, I can only guess that the problem involves communication, planning, scheduling or some combination of these things.

INTERVIEWER: (Fade up) . . . so how would you proceed?

LUIGI: My approach would be to determine whether the required production level is realistic, given the amount of equipment and workers involved. If the requirement is reasonable, then I would look for a problem on the factory line. In my experience, it has usually come down to either equipment failures due to improper maintenance or inefficient production methods. Either can usually be fixed without too much trouble.

INTERVIEWER: (Fade up) . . . can get a little disruptive.

DAGMAR: That's true, but in a situation such as this, I concentrate on the performance problem and don't let it become an issue of conflicting personalities. The employee either has acceptable performance or is dealt with according to company policy for underperforming.

Unit 10—Listening
Student Text Page 97

(Taped operator's voice.)

Hello. You have reached Cook Community College. If you are calling from a touch tone phone, you can obtain class schedule information by using your phone dial.

For information, regarding vocational classes, press 1. For information, about GED and ESL classes, press 2. For information about Continuing Education classes, press 3. You may press 0 for assistance. Press the number of your choice now.

(Tone from number 1 being pressed.)

SPEAKER: Vocational classes. Medical Assistant classes meet for 2 hours on Monday, Wednesday, and Friday at 4pm and 7pm.

If you need information about other classes, press another number now.

(Tone from number 2 being pressed.)

SPEAKER: ESL and GED classes. GED classes meet for 2 hours on Tuesday and Thursday for 3 hours beginning at either 4pm or 7pm. ESL classes meet 4 days a week, Monday through Thursday from . . . (fade out).

Skills Index

The skills listed below are introduced and/or emphasized on the pages indicated.

Cooperative Learning Skills

Group or pair work, 1, 5, 7, 10, 12, 13, 14, 15, 18, 19, 20, 21, 23, 24, 25, 26, 27, 31, 33, 34, 35, 38, 39, 42, 46, 48, 49, 51, 54, 55, 56, 57, 59, 60, 64, 66, 67, 68, 70, 71, 73, 76, 78, 79, 82, 84, 85, 86, 88, 89, 91, 95, 96

Information gap activity, 19–20

Roleplays, 15, 23, 34, 46, 56, 68, 76, 85

Critical and Creative Thinking Skills

Critical thinking, 5, 14, 25, 26, 27, 29, 34, 35, 36, 40–41, 56, 57, 58, 60, 69, 71, 76, 84, 85, 86, 87

Classification, 46

Clarifying problems, 58

Differentiation (fact vs. opinion), 5

Evaluation, 35, 36

Sequencing, 14, 16

Creative Thinking, *see roleplays, discussion and writing activities*

Functional Literacy Skills

Reading at Work, 7, 17, 27, 37, 47, 59, 70, 78, 88, 96

Bank statement, 50

Chart of reported occupational accidents and injuries, 29

Dental plan, 5

Employee suggestion form, 48

Flow chart, 56

Insurance statements, 8, 9

Laboratory information card, 19, 20

Organizational chart, 49

Production record data sheet, 79

Report of employee injury form, 28

Work schedule, 19, 20

Listening Skills

Math/Graphical Literacy Skills

Reading Comprehension Skills

Literal

Checking literal comprehension, 4, 7, 13, 17, 24, 27, 34, 38, 45, 48, 55, 59, 67, 70, 75, 78, 84, 94

Establishing prior knowledge, 1, 10, 21, 31, 42, 51, 64, 73, 82, 91

Learning and using new words, phrases and idioms, 3, 7, 12, 17, 23, 27, 33, 37, 44, 47, 54, 59, 66, 70, 75, 78, 84, 88, 93, 96

Reading and using words in a work-related vocabulary, 7, 17, 27, 37, 47, 59, 70, 78, 88, 96

Inferential

Checking inferential comprehension, 7, 13, 17, 24, 27, 34, 38, 45, 48, 59, 67

Making predictions, 1, 25, 51

Speaking Skills

Before You Read, 1, 10, 21, 31, 42, 51, 64, 73, 82, 91

Discussing *(using spoken language)*, 14, 25, 34, 46, 56, 68, 76, 85, 95

Grapevine Activity, 39

Information gap activity, 19–20

Understanding the Reading *(from Reading at Work)*, 7, 17, 27, 38, 48, 59, 70, 78, 88, 96

Writing Skills

Using written language to communicate on the job, 6, 16, 26, 48, 77

Using written language to express opinions and ideas, 36, 58, 69, 87, 98